The

Quest

For Strength and Knowledge

Psalm 27:1b *"The Lord is the strength of my life; of whom shall I be afraid? "* **NKJV**

Proverbs 1:7 *"The fear of the Lord is the beginning of knowledge . . ."* **NKJV**

By

Danny G. Thomas

FWB
For Worthwhile Books Publications
Columbus, Ohio

This book is dedicated to
Mika Sasaki,
Nomura's,
Mastamura,
And the missionaries and pastors
Along with many others, I have met in Japan.

They represent
Those who are both believers and seekers alike.

They represent the young,
The old, and those in between.
They represent those who are on
A quest for knowledge and strength in life—
Those who eagerly search
For truth, wisdom,
And understanding of life.
All of that is found in the Word of God.

Think about these things. *Selah*

Danny G. Thomas

Introduction

Psalm 119:11 KJV tells us, "Thy word have I hid in my heart, that I might not sin against thee."

Psalm 19:14 KJV informs us, "Let the words of my mouth, and the meditation of my heart, be acceptable in thy sight . . . ."

To hide God's Word is to memorize it where it cannot be taken away. Out of the mouth proceed the thoughts and intents of the heart **(Luke 6:45)**.

Therefore, a believer must have the Word of God hidden or written in his heart where he can dwell upon it daily and in various life situations. Situations summon the Word of God and keep us close to God. God's word is a refiner, a reprover, a teacher, and a guard **(2 Timothy 3:16)**.

The purpose of this devotional book is to help write God's Word in your heart, to plant it there and let it grow. I have chosen what many consider the top 90 memory verses, and for the next ninety days we will consider them, think about them, and hide them in our heart.

Think about it. *Selah*

Table of Contents

Day Thirty-four:	Psalm 23:5
Day Thirty-five:	James 1:2
Day Thirty-six:	Psalm 1:6
Day Thirty-seven:	Joshua 1:8
Day Thirty-eight:	Psalm 1:5
Day Thirty-nine:	Psalm 1:4
Day Forty:	Jeremiah 29:11
Day Forty-one:	2 Timothy 3:17
Day Forty-two:	James 1:3
Day Forty-three:	Acts 20:24
Day Forty-four:	Hebrews 4:12
Day Forty-five:	Romans 8:1
Day Forty-six:	John 3:17
Day Forty-seven:	Hebrews 11:1
Day Forty-eight:	James 1:4
Day Forty-nine:	James 1:5
Day Fifty:	John 1:2
Day Fifty-one:	Matthew 5:16
Day Fifty-two:	Matthew 5:3
Day Fifty-three:	Deuteronomy 6:5
Day Fifty-four:	Ephesians 2:10
Day Fifty-five:	Romans 10:9
Day Fifty-six:	Matthew 5:6
Day Fifty-seven:	Exodus 14:14
Day Fifty-eight:	Matthew 5:4
Day Fifty-nine:	Matthew 5:5
Day Sixty:	Matthew 5:7
Day Sixty-one:	Matthew 5:8
Day Sixty-two:	Genesis 1:2
Day Sixty-three:	John 15:7
Day Sixty-four:	Galatians 5:16
Day Sixty-five:	Joshua 1:9
Day Sixty-six:	Matthew 5:9
Day Sixty-seven:	Romans 8:39
Day Sixty-eight:	2 Timothy 1:7

Day Sixty-nine:	John 1:3
Day Seventy:	Exodus 20:3
Day Seventy-one:	Matthew 5:10
Day Seventy-two:	Isaiah 40:31
Day Seventy-three:	Ephesians 6:11
Day Seventy-four:	Romans 8:38
Day Seventy-five:	Psalm 19:14
Day Seventy-six:	Philippians 3:8
Day Seventy-seven:	Ephesians 6:10
Day Seventy-eight:	Colossians 3:23
Day Seventy-nine:	Ephesians 6:12
Day Eighty:	John 1:12
Day Eighty-one:	Philippians 3:7
Day Eighty-two:	Matthew 5:11
Day Eighty-three:	Exodus 20:12
Day Eighty-four:	Titus 1:2
Day Eighty-five:	Deuteronomy 6:4
Day Eighty-six:	Titus 1:1
Day Eighty-seven:	Ephesians 6:23
Day Eighty-eight:	Deuteronomy 6:7
Day Eighty-nine:	Genesis 2:1
Day Ninety:	Exodus 20:8

Day One: John 3:16

"For God so loved the world that He gave His only begotten Son, that whoever believes in Him should not perish but have everlasting life." **John 3:12 NKJV**

The best-known verse in the Bible is **John 3:16**. We see it displayed everywhere, at sports games, on billboards, on walls, in bathrooms and in many other places. **John 3:16** is the measuring stick of the love of God, Agape Love, unconditional love.

His love is measured by the extent that He went to offer a loving future to anyone who would take Him up on His offer of eternal life. He offers it in exchange for our future of eternal death.

It doesn't say that He would love us "if" but that He loves us, and so He came. It doesn't say that He would love us if we measure up, but that He loves us so much that, even while we were still sinners, He died for us, **Romans 5:8**. God made the first move in expressing His love—He loved us first, **1 John 4:19**.

God's expression of love was to give the best that He had and that was His only begotten Son, Jesus Christ. This was the fulfillment of a promise that He made to mankind after he disobeyed His command in **Genesis 3:15**.

God the Father makes this offer and presents this Good News. The "if" is not about His love, because He is "not willing that any should perish but that all should come to repentance," **2 Peter 3:9 KJV**. The condition in this statement is "<u>what is required to receive eternal life</u>"

and that condition is "whoever believes," <u>trusts in</u>, <u>repents.</u> Repentance is <u>turning around</u> or making a turn-a-round, a change in the direction in one's life; it is a change in one's trust factor. It is when a person realizes that he is totally unable to meet the demands of God, and he takes God up on His offer of making him acceptable or righteous enough. God offers to make the repentant one a new creation and puts on him the righteousness of His own Son, Jesus Christ, in return for putting the sin of the old creation on Jesus, **2 Corinthians 5:21**.

This is totally a God thing. It is all His idea and all His doing; we have nothing to do with the process other than to receive Him by the faith that He provides as well, **Ephesians 2:8-9**.

This is what Jesus was telling Nicodemus about in **John 3:16** and what He is saying to you as well. He is rich in mercy, full of grace, and great in love. *"But God being rich in mercy, because of the great love with which he loved us, even when we were dead in our trespasses, made us alive together with Christ—by grace you have been saved."* **Ephesians 2:4-5 ESV**

Think about it. *Selah*

Day Two: Genesis 1:1

"In the beginning, God created the heavens and the earth." **Genesis 1:1 ESV**

The beginning of time, when was that? The Bible tells us that before the beginning there was God. God was the prime mover of time. Before there was anything, there was God and He started all things. **John 1:3 ESV** says, *"All things were made through him, and without him was not anything made that was made."* That really says it all. Nothing existed in this world or universe until God moved.

We argue over the statement, *"Which came first the chicken or the egg?"* This verse in the Bible tells us the answer: The chicken came first when God created it from nothing. The tree came before the seed, the fish came first, and man came first. All things were ***created***, perfectly formed by God, and they did not evolve. God created all of the stars and the planets, everything: gravity, air, the atom, the cell and every minuscule element of life and creation all the way to its most infinitesimal part. God created it all, complete in its element. Why? Because God is good and He can do nothing that is not perfect and clean.

God is a God of order and all of creation shouts His name, responds to His command, and remains as he designed them.

"In the beginning, God created the heavens and the earth." **Genesis 1:1 ESV**
What is there that is not answered here? God did it all and He says, *"It is good."* Think about it. *Selah*

Day Three: Exodus 20:3

"You shall have no other gods before me." **Exodus 20:3 ESV**

Perhaps the greatest reason for all problems in all of humanity is this: The gods in people's lives that contradict everything of God Himself. The lowercase *god* is something that one puts before God Himself, something that take precedence over God. These "gods" stand out before the very presence of God and shout blasphemy to Him, such as: "We are God, not you, or we are God as you are God." Isn't that what Satan said? *"I will make myself like the Most High."* **Isaiah 14:14b ESV**

We can have all kinds of gods; they can be people, family, automobiles, activities, education, or anything we create in our lives that we put in place of God. God makes our lives joyful but gods make our lives happy. Happiness is conditional and can be fleeting when things in our lives are not as we would have them to be. Joy stands alone, and it has the bi-product of happiness. Storms cannot shake joy, disease cannot quench joy, and death is unable to unseat joy. Nothing can shake the joy that is in Christ Jesus because He is our joy, and in Him there is no cause for fear. Our hope, our faith, our life, and our strength are all in Him. He is able to do so much more than we could even dream of and supplies our needs abundantly according to His riches in heaven, **Philippians 4:19**. We can do all things through Him, **Philippians 4:13**

Therefore, if you want to be happy, be joyful, and if you want to be joyful, have no other gods before your God.
Think about it. *Selah*

Day Four: Philippians 4:6

"Do not be anxious about anything, but in everything by prayer and supplication with thanksgiving let your requests be made known to God." **Philippians 4:6 ESV**

Anxiety attacks. Have you ever experienced one? I have a friend who has them when she crosses a bridge. The fear that grips her mind supersedes all that she knows. Anxiety will cause one to go to great extents in order to avoid facing that fear. What is needed to overcome an anxiety is to find a help that is greater than anxiety. A confidence that can be substituted and take the place of that fear.

Paul tells us that we can overcome all our anxieties by praying and making our concerns known to God and allowing our sufficient God to counteract them or balance them out by what we know He can do. Eugene Peterson puts it this way in **The Message,** *"Don't fret or worry. Instead of worrying, pray. Let petitions and praises shape your worries into prayers . . . ."* **(Philippians 4:6)**

Bobby McFerrin's song, "Don't Worry Be Happy," puts it in a humorous way but God puts it this way: Don't worry about anything; instead, be happy by praising me and allowing those praises to shape your life. Fretting and worry only cause you unnecessary harm. So, when anxiety pops up in your life, pray and praise God.

Think about it. *Selah*

Day Five: Romans 12:2

"Do not be conformed to this world, but be transformed by the renewal of your mind, that by testing you may discern what is the will of God, what is good and acceptable and perfect." **Romans 12:2 ESV**

All through life we are pressured to conform to the majority around us. We are pulled by the opinion of others to make decisions in our personal life based on their mindset. We call it peer pressure. As children we would say, "Everybody else is doing it."   To that statement our parents would often say, "If everybody else jumps off the cliff, would you jump off a cliff?" Now, I have said that to my children and to our grandchildren. We say, "Think for yourself."   God says to not be conformed to this world but think divinely, think heavenly, think in a transformed way, **Romans 12:1-2.** He says to let Him transform your mind and your way of thinking.   He has made us a new creation: *"Therefore, if anyone is in Christ, he is a new creation. The old has passed away; behold, the new has come,"* **2 Corinthians 5:17 ESV.** Don't be a copycat of the old.   Be the new person you have been recreated to be in Christ.

How do you accomplish this? By testing the things in life by the guidance of the Holy Spirit who is our teacher and guide.   God's ways are not man's ways, **Deuteronomy 32:4.** God does not think as we think. His thoughts are divine, not human; therefore, we ought to allow the Spirit of God to reveal God's thoughts and not be given to the thoughts of this world.

If we do this, we can be assured that our ways and our decisions are good ones and perfectly acceptable to God and profitable to us as His follower.

Think about it. *Selah*

Day Six: Galatians 2:20

"I have been crucified with Christ. It is no longer I who live, but Christ who lives in me. And the life I now live in the flesh I live by faith in the Son of God, who loved me and gave himself for me." **Galatians 2:20 ESV**

Crucifixion is a brutal means of execution that was widely used by the Persians, Greeks, Egyptians, Romans and many others. It is occasionally used even today, particularly in the Middle East. It is a slow and torturous method where the victim is tied or nailed to a wooden cross and left to hang until dead. Death came because of suffocation.

Paul says that the believer has been sentenced for sin and the sentence has been carried out by our substitute, a propitiation or atonement made for our sins by Christ. He took our place in the judgment and we took the sinless position of Jesus. **2 Corinthians 5:21 ESV** says, *"For our sake he made him to be sin who knew no sin, so that in him we might become the righteousness of God."*

Therefore the human life that we live is under the cover of and the payment of Christ who was that perfect sacrifice, making us acceptable and viewable by the Father. We are totally suited for heaven because of the sacrifice of Christ Jesus. Our faith is the hope we have and the confidence in the very Word of God being true.

What manner of love is this that a pure and holy God would express this love to us by dying and making the payment, taking the punishment and the shame for us, **1 John 3:1.**
Think about it. *Selah*

Day Seven: Romans 6:23

"For the wages of sin is death, but the free gift of God is eternal life in Christ Jesus our Lord." **Romans 6:23 ESV**

What do you do to earn a living, to make a livelihood? Do you consider it a job or a profession? Do you enjoy what you do? *"If you love what you do, you will never work a day in your life."* That is the challenge made to young people to find something that they love to do to make a living. If you love what you do, it won't be work to you. It will be a joy.

We argue about what is a fair living wage as well as the idea of what a minimum should be and even if there ought to be a minimum wage. Wages have always been something to argue about. Remember the parable of a master of a vineyard who went out early in the morning and hired laborers to work in his vineyard for an agreed day's wage. They began to work, but as the day went along the master saw others. After three hours, six hours, and even at the eleventh hour he said to all of those, I will pay you what I consider fair. At the end of the day, the master of the vineyard paid everyone the same amount of money for the day's work, not the length of time that they worked. When those who had actually worked all day grumbled to the master that the pay scale was not fair, the master's response to the grumblers complaint was, "I gave you what you asked and to the others I gave what I chose to give them, why are you begrudging my generosity?" **Matthew 20:1–16**

Humanity will continue to grumble about wages and they will continue to begrudge the generosity of the employer. Wages are given for work done. In **Romans**

6:23 the wage is used as an example to understand sin. Sin is the commodity, the product or the work done, and death is the wage for it. We do the work and we receive the pay. The payment is death. We entered into this work of sin, and we will be paid for the work. Everyone will. **Romans 3:23**

Our wages for our sins is bad news, and that bad news is eternal death for what we have done; but there is Good News and the Good News is a gift, not a wage. A gift is given because of the generosity and will of the Master. A gift is a blessing and a blessing is undeserved. Eternal life is undeserved. We don't deserve it in any way, but it is offered to all who respond to the convicting voice of the Holy Spirit as He draws them to Jesus by the Father and repent of their sin and take Jesus as their Savior, **John 6:43.** This is a gift, it is the gift of God and that gift is eternal life that Jesus Christ has paid the prince.

"For the wages of sin is death, but the gift of God is eternal life in Christ Jesus our Lord." **Romans 6:23 ESV**

Think about it. *Selah*

Day Eight: Romans 12:1

"I appeal to you therefore, brothers, by the mercies of God, to present your bodies as a living sacrifice, holy and acceptable to God, which is your spiritual worship."
Romans 12:1 ESV

To appeal is to make an urgent, open, and serious request. It is to plead with someone about some information that you have to make known. Paul is making an urgent and public request that needs to be addressed immediately and with certainty. He makes this request not to the world but to those who are believers, those who are brothers and sisters in Christ Jesus. There is something that is wrong in their lives and that something must be brought to their attention with all haste.

It has to do with their spiritual worship or the way they honor God with their lives. Mercy is not giving that which is deserved, and their lives were not being lived in a deserving way to God. It was a false worshiping life; a life that was lived by their own desires, not God's desires. Their lives were not sacrificial to God. Their lives were reflective of the world. Their lives were not showing the light of Christ but were lived in a way that was acceptable to the world. **Romans 12:2** sheds light on this lifestyle. It was conforming to the world, not transforming to God.

This spiritual worship was not spiritual at all, it was tainted by the world's way of thinking, and that was totally unacceptable to God. This lifestyle was impure and unreasonable.

This is a caution to us, and that caution is to be careful how we live and not to be influenced by the complaint of this world. The complaint is that Christianity is out of style, out of step with time, and that the world and needs change. Change is to do something different. If we are like the world, we are not different; we are the same. The world wants conformity to its way. If change comes, it will take a turning and turning is repentance. Repentance is turning around; it is making a change from the normal.

So this is the appeal: *"I appeal to you therefore, brothers, by the mercies of God, to present your bodies as a living sacrifice, holy and acceptable to God, which is your spiritual worship."* **Romans 12:1 ESV**

Think about it. *Selah*

Day Nine: Ephesians 2:8

"For by grace you have been saved through faith. And this is not your own doing; it is the gift of God." **Ephesians 2:8 ESV**

Grace is the reason that God gives for saving people. Grace is undeserved and unmerited favor. Grace along with mercy is what is behind His gift of eternal life. If you have repented of your sins and asked Jesus to step into the place where that sin took up residence, then you are a believer in Jesus, a follower of Jesus, a child of God or a Christian.

A person is able to benefit from grace because of the faith that God provided as well. Saving us is all His idea. It has all to do with what He has already done for us. Our part is to repent, believe, and to acknowledge that we are totally unable to do anything to make ourselves acceptable to God by any effort of our own.

May I ask you a question? What are you doing about your life and your eternal future? If you think you are able to make it on your own, you are wrong. If you believe anything other than what God has provided, you are sadly mistaken. If what you consider to be truth does not match up with what God has said, then, your truth is a total lie. If truth is not the whole truth, and nothing but the truth, it is a lie and there is no truth about it. Jesus tells us that He is the Truth and the Life and no man can come to the Father except through Him, The Truth, **John 14:6**.

One more thing, if you have repented of your sin and confessed that Jesus is the very Son of God and that He rose from the grave, has ascended to the Father, and will soon come again for us, then you are saved. You have that gift of eternal life, and it is all the doing of God. If Satan causes you to doubt, remember he is a liar and was one from the beginning. Jesus tells us that He is the Truth, so believe the Truth.

"For by grace you have been saved through faith. And this is not your own doing; it is the gift of God." **Ephesians 2:8 ESV**

Think about it. *Selah*

Day Ten: Philippians 4:7

"And the peace of God, which surpasses all understanding will guard your hearts and your minds in Christ Jesus." **Philippians 4:7 ESV**

The Nobel Peace Prize is one of the five medals created by the Swedish industrialist Alfred Nobel, an inventor of armaments. The five medals are awards offered by Sweden and they are awarded for the areas of Chemistry, Physics, Physiology or Medicine, Literature, and Peace. It is odd that the Peace Prize comes from the inventor of explosives and war supplies.

We seek peace but we make war. When we do reach for peace, it turns out to be such a fleeting peace or temporary peace. In this world will we ever find that true peace? Jesus said in **John 14:27** that He would leave His peace with us and it was nothing like the world's type of peace. It was that real peace. His peace goes beyond our understanding. It lasts even when it seems as though it should have come to an end. It can be observed in a time of tragedy. We see it in oppression. It sustains us in persecutions, and it will not leave us. It endures.

The peace of Christ is a wonder. Eugene Peterson paraphrases it this way: *"Before you know it, a sense of God's wholeness, everything coming together for good, will come and settle you down. It's wonderful what happens when Christ displaces worry at the center of your life."* **Philippians 4:7 *The Message***

God's peace stands guard at our heart as we sojourn through this world. This world is not our home, but we are going home. Our minds are at peace even in the worst of times. This is God's peace.

Think about it. *Selah*

Day Eleven: Romans 8:28

"And we know that for those who love God all things work together for good, for those who are called according to his purpose." **Romans 8:28 ESV**

One of the most abused verses in the Bible is **Romans 8:28**. We Christians seem to use it to battle difficulty and tragedy in our lives. We give the idea that when grief is experienced all we need to do is to just go on with life and everything will be okay; but everything isn't okay in our lives. There are things that happen that are not okay. They are part of life but this earthly life is not good. We must, however, learn how to live out that life.

Here is how we should understand this verse: Christians, the individuals who have been drawn by God, convicted by the Holy Spirit, given the faith to believe God's Word, and desire to obey God's call in their lives, can be assured that even when difficult things happen to us that were meant for evil or to cause us harm, God will step in and weave those very things into the fabric of our lives to make us stronger and better. He will develop us to be the effective tool and quality instrument that He desired us to be as we do what He has called us to do.

We can be assured that if God is for us, nothing can trump our ministry of fulfilling His purpose in our life. We can be confident of this. There is no reason to worry or lose faith because God is faithful.

"And we know that for those who love God all things work together for good, for those who are called according to his purpose." **Romans 8:28 ESV**
Think about it. *Selah*

Day Twelve: Psalm 1:1

"Blessed is the man who walks not in the counsel of the wicked, nor stands in the way of sinners, nor sits in the seat of the scoffers." **Psalm 1:1 ESV**

Blessed is the man, to be envied is the individual, who decides that he will not take counsel of the world's way of thinking. The person, who does not conform to the intellect of this world but desires to transform his thinking to please God and to do things in God's way, will discover shortly that he has made a wise decision.

Blessed is the man who does not take part in complaining with all the complainers and grumblers of this world and the schemers who are found gathering everywhere. Grumblers and complainers are losers. They are spreaders of discord, which God hates, **Proverbs 6:16-19.** Avoid the grumbler and run from the complainer; they are losers.

Blessed is the man who is not numbered along with the scoffers. Scoffers are spreaders of discord, **Proverbs 6:16-19.** Shun those who spread discord. Don't be counted among them because they are losers. Don't fall into a trap by associating with scoffers. You are a blessed man if you are careful of those you hang around.

Think about it. *Selah*

Day Thirteen: Romans 5:8

"But God showed his love for us in that while we were still sinners, Christ died for us." **Romans s 5:8 ESV**

I saw a video that a father took of his two sons, one about four years old and the other about six, and both were totally covered with paint from head to toe. "Who got into the paint?" the father asked. "No one," said the two brothers. "Well how did you get covered with paint?" They responded, "I don't know." The father then said, "Whose idea was this?" Each of the brothers pointed to the other. There was a long pause and one of the brothers started to smile. The father, who could hardly keep from laughing himself said, "This is no laughing matter." Then the father said, "Who's going to clean this up?" The brothers sheepishly pointed to each other. I laughed because it was not my boys!

The boys were guilty but the father was the one who would have to clean the paint up. The father would do it begrudgingly but would do it because he loved those two boys.

Did you know that God loves you so much that even while you were in the act of sinning and rejecting Him, He died for you? But unlike the father in the video, He did what we could not do to clean us up and make us acceptable and clean before the Father. He did it lovingly and not begrudgingly.

God proves His love to us by offering us forgiveness and the righteousness of His Son Jesus in exchange for our unrighteousness, **2 Corinthians 5:21.**
Think about it. *Selah*

Day Fourteen: Proverbs 3:5

"Trust in the Lord with all your heart, and do not lean on your own understanding." **Proverbs 3:5 ESV**

Have you ever been misunderstood? Have you ever misunderstood someone else? I would say both are true in your life. Misunderstanding is the cause of so many fights, the source of so many broken relationships and the root of bad feelings in the lives of those who used to be the best of friends.

How one sees things cannot be relied upon and there certainly can be misunderstandings when people place their confidence totally upon how things seem to be or how they appear to be. A misunderstanding is founded upon your understanding, which may be partially untrue. For something to be true it must be totally true in every aspect. Remember, if something is partially true or 99% true that makes it a total lie. The lie may not be intended but it's still untrue.

Solomon instructs the reader not to give preference to or be prejudiced toward your personal understanding. Give room for correction. For sure never make decisions or come to conclusions before taking time for consideration of all options.

The first thing that must be done is to place your trust in the Lord for guidance and to seek the insight of the Holy Spirit, who is our counselor, our teacher, and our peace. God knows all things and sees all things. In James 1:5 we are admonished to ask the Lord for wisdom in making decisions, and if we ask, He will respond—not might respond. We can depend upon God's direction in our lives. We can trust in the Lord with all our heart. He is faithful to lead and His ways are sure.

Trust is a comforting thing. *"Trust in the Lord with all your heart, and do not lean on your own understanding. In all your ways acknowledge him, and he will make straight your paths."* **Proverbs 3: 5-6 ESV**

Think about it. *Selah*

Day Fifteen: Hebrews 12:1

"Therefore, since we are surrounded by so great a cloud of witnesses, let us also lay aside every weight, and sin which clings so closely, and let us run with endurance the race that is set before us." **Hebrews 12:1 ESV**

On your mark! Get set! Go! To run a race, the runner must be conditioned, he must be focused, and he must be encouraged. You cannot run well if you have not conditioned and properly prepared yourself for that race. If you have not gone through that needed training, you will fail. A runner needs a will or a reason to run, a competent trainer or coach, and an assignment to a specific race. A runner must not only have competent people around him and a will or passion to run but he must be willing to do whatever it takes to win the race and deny himself many luxuries that would hinder or take away from his chances of winning. He must strip himself of all weights (light is right), and any other desire he might have must give way to his great desire of running and winning the race.

There is one other factor in the race—the crowd. The loud cheer from the stands summons the adrenalin rush, and it gives us added strength, strength that we did not know we had.   That great crowd of believers, the believers in God and believers in us, give us added strength. This crowd is not your ordinary crowd for they are fellow athletes who have been in a race before. They not only have been in a race, but they are victors of the race. Not only are these witnesses fellow athletes, but they are fellow believers, or brothers and sisters in Christ. They are your family and they love you. They are proud of you and stand behind you to cheer you on.

So, what is the race that has been set before you? How are you running? If you're beginning to get winded, listen to the crowd and get your second wind. You can win this one!

"Therefore, since we are surrounded by so great a cloud of witnesses, let us also lay aside every weight, and sin which clings so closely, and let us run with endurance the race that is set before us." **Hebrews 12:1 ESV**

Think about it. *Selah*

Day Sixteen: Romans 3:23

"For all have sinned and fall short of the glory of God."
Romans 3:23 ESV

No one wants to fall short of a goal, and no one wants to miss a target. No one wants to lose and fall below what they have strived to obtain. Paul is telling us in **Romans 3:23** that there is not one person who can meet up to the standard that God has set for us. The standard is perfection. God glories in His perfection because of just that fact. He stands alone in His perfection. All His created beings fall short and are hopeless to meet that standard, and this brings about a problem. The problem is how one of God's creations can hope to go to heaven while being unable to meet God's ridged standard. The way is Jesus and Jesus is the glory of the Father. Jesus meets that ridged standard well.

God glories in His glory and wants His creation to glory in Him and to accept His glorious offer of redemption. He offers glory for our sin, heaven to replace our hell, and peace for our war. In **2 Corinthians 5:21** we read that the Father has made His perfect and glorious Son, Jesus, to be our sin in order that we could be made the righteousness of God or the glory of God.

Are you trying to meet the standard of God? Quit trying because you cannot do it. If you think you have met that standard, then once again you have missed the target. You have fallen woefully short and are without hope in yourself. Only Jesus can meet that standard for you.

"For all have sinned and fall short of the glory of God."
Romans 3:23 ESV

Think about it. *Selah*

Day Seventeen: Proverbs 3:6

"In all your ways acknowledge him, and he will make straight your paths."
Proverbs 3:6 ESV

I have a GPS for my car and it is a great asset to me while driving, most of the time. There have been many occasions where it was trying to lead me down a path that I did not want to go and asking me to turn onto a road that was not there. It is a good device most of the time, as long as I have read an actual road map.

I have received directions from individuals and they were generally good. At times they would say, *"When you come to a fork in the road, turn left,"* or *"Look for a white fence and we are across the street."* If I missed the sign, I found myself lost.

Solomon is advising us to acknowledge God for direction in our road of life. He tells us that if we acknowledge Him as we go, our path will be right and straight. **Isaiah 30:21** tells us to listen to the voice and guidance of the Lord in our life, and He will give us specific and correct directions in the way we should go. **James 1:5** encourages us to ask God for advice when we lack the wisdom, when we want to do what is right, and to make the difficult decisions in life. We can trust Him to answer us and to help us in those times. He doesn't say He *might* give us direction. He says that He *will* and He does not show favoritism.

God is the perfect GPS, and He does not lead you down the wrong road. He makes your path straight and perfect. So, consult God in your decision-making, trust

His Word at all times, and respond to His voice and His leading.

   "In all your ways acknowledge him, and he will make straight your paths."
Proverbs 3:6 ESV

   Think about it. *Selah*

Day Eighteen: Philippians 4:8

"Finally, brothers, whatever is true, whatever is honorable, whatever is just, whatever is pure, whatever is lovely, whatever is commendable, if there is any excellence, if there is anything worthy of praise, think about these things." **Philippians 4:8 ESV**

The saying goes, "An idol mind is the devil's workshop." And that is true. Empty space gathers dust and a rolling stone gathers no moss. One of the difficulties that we all will experience from time to time is finding ourselves in situations where we feel we have nothing to do. When we have nothing to do, Satan has a hay-day.

There are also times when we allow individuals of less worth to infiltrate our thinking to share their evil or worthless thoughts, thoughts that tear down rather than build up, and we become as they are.

Here in Philippians 4:8, Paul gives us some good advice and that is to filter our mind and only think of things of worth and praise. Isn't that what Jesus did and what He asks us to do as His messengers of Good News? Do away with bad news and strengthen others with thoughts that are true and factual, not false or questionable. Think about things that honor others rather than those that dishonor. He encourages us to be upright and justified in our thought process rather than vindictive and judgmental. We should have pure thoughts that honor God in the place of dirty and damaging thoughts. We should strive to be altogether lovely and not hateful. We should seek out and find commendable thoughts that edify others, God, and ourselves. Paul continues with an added qualifier, and that is, if these things seem to be things of excellence and praiseworthy, and of course they are, then make these thoughts your thoughts.

We have been commissioned as bearers of Good News, God's Good News. We are the witnesses of Jesus and not of the world and its prince. It takes an aggressive effort to think good thoughts while we are pressured to think thoughts of this world, so be a good ambassador of Christ Jesus. The world needs this Good News.

"Therefore brothers, whatever is true, whatever is honorable, whatever is just, whatever is pure, whatever is lovely, whatever is commendable, if there is any excellence, if there is anything worthy of praise, think about these things."
Ephesians 4:8 ESV

Think about it. *Selah*

Day Nineteen: Psalm 1:2

"But his delight is the law of the Lord, and on his law he meditates day and night." **Psalm 1:2 ESV**

Ignorance of the law is no excuse. I've heard that saying pretty much all my life. To obey the law and not break the law suggests that one must learn the law.

David writes in Psalm 1 that a blessed man is a man that not only knows the law but understands what the law means, what the law requires, and what the penalty for breaking the law is. When an individual understands why a law is a law, he then finds that that law is a blessing to him and, therefore, he takes delight in that law.

Day and night this blessed man thinks about this law. He understands that this law is not an unjust law because it is the law of the Lord, the Good Shepherd that he writes about in **Psalm 23**. It is the law of the Lord God Almighty who is mighty to save. It is the law of the One who is our Rock and Savior, our Protector, our Strong Defense, our Shelter, a Friend that sticks closer than a brother, our Joy, our Heart's Desire, our Guide and so much more. When we think on the laws that He has written for us, we take joy in those laws. We know those laws, and it is not difficult to follow His law. We enjoy thinking about His law, and our thoughts cause us to understand that we are of all people, most blessed.

"But his delight is the law of the Lord, and on his law he meditates day and night."
Psalm 1:2 ESV

Think about it. *Selah*

Day Twenty: Galatians 5:22 & 23

"But the fruit of the Spirit is love, joy, peace, patience, kindness, goodness, faithfulness, gentleness, self-control; against such things there is no law."
Galatians 5:22-23 ESV

I love fruit, especially fresh fruit. I love going into the market and smelling the good fruit and vegetables that are there on display to be sold. My wife and I enjoy going to a local farm, Brown's Farm, to pick up some peaches, watermelon, peas, beans, and corn.   Fresh fruits and vegetables are a delightful joy to our lives.

Fresh fruits are good for the body and the mind. In the same manner, spiritual fruits are good for everyone. There is no law that prevents one from eating good, well-grown, and delicious and mouth-watering fruit.

The believer or follower of Christ Jesus is encouraged to partake of this product of the Holy Spirit. One of the benefits of the Holy Spirit is good fruit. When we are listening and abiding with the Holy Spirit, we bear Spiritual fruit. It is the fruit of the Spirit that associates us with the Holy Spirit. It is not necessary for believers to tell others that they are Christians because they look and smell like a follower of Jesus Christ.

So, this is the challenge: Allow others to see that good fruit that hangs from you, as you are a partaker and a beneficiary of the fruit of the Spirit. Now, what does your life look like? Is your fruit fresh, or has it fallen to the ground and begun to rot? Stay fresh, stay connected to the tree, and allow others to benefit from that fresh fruit of the Spirit.

"But the fruit of the Spirit is love, joy, peace, patience, kindness, goodness, faithfulness, gentleness, self-control; against such things there is no law."
Galatians 5:22-23 ESV

Think about it. *Selah*

Day Twenty-one: Psalms 119:11

"I have stored up your word in my heart that I might not sin against you." **Psalm 119:11 ESV**

Memorizing the Word of God is one of the most beneficial things that a believer in God can do. To have instant access to the very Word of God at any moment will keep one close to God because he has the mind of God in his mind. It is in **James 4:8** we read that if we draw near to God, He will draw near to us. Where God is, Satan does not want to be. Perhaps I could more correctly say, where God is acknowledged, praised, worshipped and adored, Satan does not want to be present. We know God is everywhere at all times, but Satan is not. Satan knows that, but he does not want to be where God is loved and adored because he is a God hater. He disobeys God and his desire is to encourage as many as possible to disobey as well.

What David is saying in this verse is be prepared and have nourishment and protection close at hand in the event of an attack, similar to those people who are preparing for world war and have bomb shelters filled with supplies and weapons to be used in the event of an attack. Paul tells us in **Ephesians 6:10 – 20** that we are already in a battle, and that we ought to do all that needs to be done to be prepared to take our stand for God.

No one can take what you have memorized because it is hidden in your mind, and it is effective and accessible.

"I have stored up your word in my heart that I might not sin against you." **Psalm 119:11 ESV**
Think about it. *Selah*

Day Twenty-two: 2 Timothy 3:16

"All Scripture is breathed out by God and profitable for teaching, for reproof, for correction, and for training in righteousness, that the man of God may be complete, equipped for every good work." **2 Timothy 3:16 ESV**

The inspiration of Scripture is fundamental to the believer's obeying God. It is God's voice to him. If the believer doubts that Scripture is the actual Word of the living God, he cannot be obedient or pleasing to God. The theological term for inspiration means that Scripture (the original manuscripts of the Bible) is the *"plenary verbal"* inspired Word of God, that is, the very God-breathed, word-for-word inspired Word of God.   It means that the Holy Spirit moved the men of old to write using their own manner of writing and vocabulary to relate the very Word of God. **2 Peter 1:20-21** puts it this way in the **New Living Translation**: *"Above all, you must realize that no prophecy in Scripture ever came from the prophet's own understanding, or from human initiative. No, those prophets were moved by the Holy Spirit, and they spoke from God."*

Paul is saying this to Timothy here in **2 Timothy 3:16**. All Scripture is the actual breath of God to us, and it is the basis for our message and the making of disciples. It is profitable and reliable to be used in teaching other believers God's desire for them in life, how they should act, and that they should be a witness to others and a carrier of God's Good News.   The believer can be confident that Scripture is not a man's understanding of God but God's written Word to all believers.

We must remember that Scripture is not written to unbelievers; it is written to believers. It is His love letter to his children. It is used to teach, to reprimand, to make correction where mistakes have been made, and it is the Manual for living a righteous life. By living a righteous life, we are an example to others and are confident and completely equipped to do everything that God may ask us to do.

All of Scripture is God's Word. Every bit of it is God-breathed and can be counted upon. Scripture does not just contain the Word of God within its pages. All of it is His voice and no other.

If you are a believer and a follower of Jesus, Scripture is God's Word to you. If you read it, the Holy Spirit will cause you to understand it. You do not need to rely on any other. Jesus left the Comforter, the Holy Spirit, to teach us and remind us. Why would you ask someone to explain what God means in His letter to you when He wants to tell you Himself? Read, listen, and learn.

"All Scripture is breathed out by God and profitable for teaching, for reproof, for correction, and for training in righteousness, that the man of God may be complete, equipped for every good work." **2 Timothy 3:16 ESV**

Think about it. *Selah*

Day Twenty-three: Philippians 4:13

"I can do all things through Christ who strengthens me."
Philippians 4:13 NKJV

Are you having difficulty living the Christian life? Are there some things that you feel that God would have you do but you just don't think you are able to do them? Do you feel defeated, hindered or strained? If any of these things are true for you, then let's step back and see what is happening.

Did you know that God would never ask you to do something other than what He would fully equip you and empower you to achieve? Well, it is the truth and there is no exception to the statement that I have just made. Did you know that Jesus Himself stands behind His word, He is the voice of Truth, He is the Truth, and He cannot lie?

Jesus never intended for you to do anything on your own. As a matter of fact, He is disappointed when you try to do things on your own because you will fail doing them on your own. If you think you are strong enough to do something on your own, then it will be your strength that will cause you to fail. Only when you feel incompetent and insufficient will God take all of those weaknesses and add to them His strength. By His strength alone victory will come. **2 Corinthians 12:10**

So, what is it that God would have you to do? Whatever that is, do it. You can do all things through Christ Jesus our Lord.

"I can do all things through Christ who strengthens me."
Philippians 4:13 NKJV

Think about it. *Selah*

Day Twenty-four: Psalm 23:1

"The Lord is my shepherd; I shall not want." **Psalm 23:1 ESV**

Everyone likes to have a helper, a guide and a protector. A helper, guide and protector is someone who either is charged with or has taken upon himself the duty of watching out for someone other than himself. A shepherd is just that. A shepherd cares for the sheep or he shepherds the sheep.

David grew up as a shepherd boy and knew well the duty and challenge that a shepherd has. A shepherd is not a hired person but an owner of the sheep. In **John 10:14,** Jesus says that He knows His sheep and His sheep know His voice and respond to His voice **(John 10:4).** The believers are His sheep and the sheep of His pasture **(Psalm 100:3).**

God (The Lord) is not just an ordinary shepherd but He is the Good Shepherd. He knows all about His sheep. He doesn't just care for His sheep but He goes exceeding abundantly above what is required for caring for His sheep **(Ephesians 3:20).** There will never be a time that His sheep are not well taken care of, and He goes above and beyond what is necessary and supplies according to His riches in heaven by Christ Jesus our Shepherd **(Philippians 4:19).**

"The Lord is my shepherd; I shall not want," **Psalm 23:1 ESV.** Be confident throughout life for The Lord is your Shepherd, The Lord who is mighty to save, and The Lord who is our strength, our light, and our comfort.
Think about it. *Selah*

Day Twenty-five: Ephesians 2:9

". . . not a result of works, so that no one may boast."
Ephesians 2:9 ESV

Are you proud of your work? Do you get satisfaction from seeing a finished product of your own? There is a sense of pride that goes with a work that is well done. Excellence is something that most people strive to achieve. Many times we fail, but when we do reach that goal of perfection, we stand back with pride, a pride that is well deserved.

The believer is the creation of Jesus Christ, the desire of the Father, and the polishing of the Holy Spirit. This work of God is well beyond the capabilities of any creation. Only the Creator is able to do this work, and He is glorified for it. We magnify Him because of it.

There is no human being or heavenly being who can take credit for that work. It is God's and God's alone. God alone thought of this idea, God made the plans for the completion of that divine idea, and God alone can boast of the results of that idea. His work lasts for eternity. It is unconditionally guaranteed and backed by His Seal of approval, which is the Holy Spirit. His work gives Him great pleasure and all that pleasure belongs solely to Him.

". . . not a result of works, so that no one may boast."
Ephesians 2:9 ESV

Think about it. *Selah*

Day Twenty-six: John 1:1

"In the beginning was the Word, and the Word was with God, and the Word was God." **John 1:1 ESV**

John 1 and **Genesis 1** go together: *"In the beginning, God created the heavens and the earth"* and *"In the beginning was the Word, and the Word was with God and the Word was God."* The Biblical fact is that God created the heavens and the earth and Jesus (The Word) was there with Him (The Father). Genesis tells us, *"And God said."* His voice is His word and his Word is Jesus.

Jesus is the Only Begotten Son of God **(John 3:16).** Jesus was sent to humanity, His creation, to bring some *"new"* news and the *"new"* news is the Good News, which is that Jesus came to pay the price for the fallen creation of God.

Because Jesus was there with the Father at the creation gives Him credibility. He is the very Word of God the Father, and God the Father calls the Word his Son. He is the Breath of Life. He breathed into His creation the breath of life and man became a living soul **(Genesis 2:7).**

So God created not only man, but all that was created was created only by God. Nothing evolved. It was created. Everything was created by God and by His voice. Creation came as a response to His voice. God said, and it was. This was a Trinity thing. The whole Godhead was involved, all three: God the Father, God the Son or the Word of God, and God the Holy Spirit. As is recorded in **Genesis 1:26** *"Let us make man in our image, after our likeness . . . ."*

"In the beginning was the Word, and the Word was with God, and the Word was God." **John 1:1 ESV**

Think about it. *Selah*

Day Twenty-seven: Psalm 1:3

"He is like a tree planted by streams of water that yields its fruit in its season, and its leaf does not wither. In all that he does, he prospers." **Psalm 1:3 ESV**

A good gardener doesn't just plant things; he plans his garden. He knows the plants that he desires to plant and purposefully places them where they can mature and where they have all that is needed to not only grow, but to grow to be the fruitful plants that they are meant to be.

A fruit tree requires much water if it is to be strong and produce good fruit.   Water is a major thing for the tree. The roots of the tree need to have access to that life-giving water. If there is no water, the tree will die.

One of the outward signs of a healthy tree is green leaves. The leaves give witness to all that may pass by that there will be fruit soon. When the flowers of the tree bloom, it gives witness that the fruit has begun its maturing process. The leaves give glory to the tree, the flower gives witness of the budding fruit, and the fruit honors the gardener who took the time to place it where it would have the greatest opportunity to grow and produce fruit.

The believer is the tree planted by God and that believer gives witness to God. There is an old Gospel Song whose refrain says, *"Brighten the corner where you are."* When God plants us, we ought to drink of the water where He has planted us and wait for the spiritual fruit to come so that we can be a blessing to those who are around us. When we do that, we will soon experience the good hand of God using us and causing us to be fruitful in

His service. Being a prosperous tree is being a fruitful tree, and a fruitful tree has within it the seed of new life. That life is eternal life that will create other trees; or as Jesus told his disciples, *"Go and make disciples."* **(Matthew 28:19-20)**

"He is like a tree planted by streams of water that yields its fruit in its season, and its leaf does not wither. In all that he does, he prospers." **Psalm 1:3 ESV**

Think about it. *Selah*

Day Twenty-eight: 2 Corinthians 5:17

"Therefore, if anyone is in Christ, he is a new creation. The old has passed away; behold, the new has come." **1 Corinthians 5:17 ESV**

Did you know that you are a creation of God? The reason you are here on this earth is because you are a creation of God. God is the Creator and we are His creation. Something happened after God created this earth and that was sin. Sin polluted God's creation and He developed a new plan that would show just how marvelous and glorious that our God is. Jesus, God's only begotten Son, would be used to display the extent that He would go in His desire to make wrong right.

We read in Genesis 1 that God's creation act was good and very good. But the new creation, the new earth, and the new heaven would be way beyond the old creation to visualize. This is a Creator thing, performed with Creator understanding. The old has passed away and everything has become a new creation. It is all brand new.

Are you a new creation? You can be.

Think about it. *Selah*

Day Twenty-nine: Psalm 23:6

"Surely goodness and mercy shall follow me all the days of my life, and I shall dwell in the house of the Lord forever. **Psalm 23:6 ESV**

It was the thief on the cross who asked Jesus to remember him when he came into his new Kingdom. Jesus' response to him was, *"Today you will be with me in paradise."* **(Luke 23:43)**

How is it that we are able to enter the Kingdom of God? Jesus first says that we can count on goodness and we can count on righteousness if we are with Him. Remember the response of Jesus to the rich young ruler in **Mark 10:18?** The young man ran up to Jesus, bowed before Him, and called Jesus Good Master. Jesus said, why do you call me good? There is only one good and that is God. We also read in **Psalm 14:3** that there is none that is good. In **Romans 3:10,** we read that there is none that is righteous, not even one person. Actually there is one righteous and that is Jesus.

This goodness and righteousness is found in Jesus. If Jesus is with you, you have His righteousness upon you, and that makes you good **(2 Corinthians 5:21).** Because of this, you are a recipient of God's mercy. It also follows you, and you will be able to live forever in heaven with Jesus in the house of our Lord.

The goodness of Jesus and His mercy follow us all throughout our life here on earth, and then we live in His house forever. Amen

Think about it. *Selah*

Day Thirty: Psalm 23:4

"Even though I walk through the valley of the shadow of death, I will fear no evil, for you are with me; your rod and your staff, they comfort me." **Psalm 23:4 ESV**

What is it about death that bothers us? More likely than not, what bothers us is the unknown. What is it that is on the other side of death? What the Psalmist tells us is that there is a guide and a Shepherd leading His sheep, He knows the other side, and He has prepared a place or pasture for His sheep. In **2 Corinthians 5,** Paul writes that our earthly body is a temporary place. What we have is a tent, a temporary house, but He has prepared for us a permanent dwelling. Jesus told His disciples that in **John 14.**

What I am saying is that the believer in Jesus has no need for fear because he is in the care of Jesus. Jesus has prepared for the believer's provision and for his protection. Jesus can be trusted, and if He can be trusted, there is no fear even in the very shadow of death.

What about you? Are you afraid of death? There is no need to be afraid if you are in Jesus.

Think about it. *Selah*

Day Thirty-one: Psalm 23:2

"He makes me lie down in green pastures. He leads me beside still waters. He restores my soul." **Psalm 23:2-3 ESV**

"It's time for your nap. But I don't want to take a nap! I know you don't want to take a nap but you need to take one." This is a conversation that most all parents have had with one or more of their children. Taking a nap is not something that children want to take time out of their busy schedule to do; but they need a nap and most of the time their mother needs that time as well.

As we get older, naptime is something that is treasured by us who are fortunate enough to have achieved the title of middle age or older. Children need their nap to help them deal with life and to restore, reset or refocus them emotionally and re-energize them physically. They don't realize this, but the parents do and they make them lie down for a while. They may cry or throw a tantrum, but a good parent will make them lie down.

The same is true with the Great Shepherd. He often has to make us lie down in pleasant pastures, although we do not want to and may question Him and throw our tantrum. He makes us lie down and lie down in green pastures, or a pleasant comfortable place, and He causes our souls to rest; that is, *"He makes me lie down in green pastures. He leads me beside still waters."* He turns on the sound machine and we hear that comforting sound of water falling and running over the rocks. He causes us to be at peace. He brings us a glass of water. Soon we forget about things, and our eyes close as we gently fall asleep

71

before the Good Shepherd. Our Shepherd knows His sheep and He prepares for them and protects them. He comforts His people.

Have you ever come to a place in your life where you questioned God for pressing the pause button in your life? Have you wondered why some things happen in your life that seem to make no sense to you? Are there places that you want to go, things that you want to do, and people that you want to see but God says, *"It's time for your nap?"* Don't question God. Just lie down in the green pasture and rest for a while. When you wake up, you will be restored.

"He makes me lie down in green pastures. He leads me beside still waters. He restores my soul." **Psalm 23:2-3 ESV**

God knows His sheep, and though you don't want to take a nap, it's time for your nap.

Think about it. *Selah*

Day Thirty-two: Psalm 23:3

"He restores my soul. He leads me in paths of righteousness for his name's sake." **Psalm 23:3 ESV**

Every now and then your computer, mobile phone, or iPad has a need to be restored or to rest for it to run efficiently and run at its maximum capacity. If you have not downloaded the required updates, you will experience unnecessary problems because you have not restored it.

The believer needs the same restoration, or refreshing time, if he is to be the witness that God has made him to be. Things just go wrong if you don't restore or refresh on a regular basis.

The believer needs the gentle guidance of the Holy Spirit and the encouragement of fellow believers to be the witness he should be.

Did you know you have on you the name of God, and you are His new creation if you have repented of your sin and asked Jesus to be your Lord and Savior? People expect you to be different because of whose you are. We are to act differently because we *are* different, and God is not glorified when we operate as those who do not know Him as Savior and Lord.

The Holy Spirit is our guide as well as our seal of approval of God, and He will not lead us in ways that are in direct conflict with His righteousness. God leads us for our best interest and for His righteousness' sake. We can rest in the fact that He will lead us and lead us well, because He is righteous. *"He restores my soul. He leads me in paths of righteousness for his name's sake."* **Psalm 23:3 ESV**

Think about it. *Selah*

Day Thirty-three: 1 John 1:9

"If we confess our sins, he is faithful and just to forgive us our sins and to cleanse us from all unrighteousness."
1 John 1:9 ESV

Alexander Pope wrote in his <u>Essay on Criticism Part 2</u>:

> *"Ah ne're a thirst of glory boast,*
> *nor in the critic let man be lost!*
> *Good-nature and good-sense must never join;*
> *to err is human; to forgive Divine."*

Sin is a part of mankind. To live in this world is to sin in this world. We have a sinful nature. This is why Jesus came into this world. He came to give us a new nature in Him and a divine nature in Him. To sin is human and, thanks to God, only He can forgive sin. He came to do just that.   Jesus came to offer us His righteousness in exchange for our sin **(2 Corinthians 5:21)**.

Forgiveness is reserved for God alone, and the Pharisees acknowledged that fact in **Mark 2:7**. Forgiveness can come only by the one wronged; and when we sin, we sin against God for all sin is against God.

The good news is that God wants to forgive us of sin and He expressed it by sending His only Son Jesus. Even while we were still sinners, dead in our sin and actively involved in our sinning, Jesus paid the price for our sins **(Romans 5:8, Ephesians 2:5)**.

Therefore, because God is the only one who can forgive sin, only He has the right to forgive, and Jesus has justified that action of forgiveness. He requires that we ask for forgiveness. We must humble ourselves to the point where we bow before Him and seek His forgiveness. At that point He will forgive us our sin; and it is right and just for Him to forgive those sins.

What we get in exchange for our sin is the righteousness of Jesus, the holiness of Jesus, the purity of Jesus, and the right to stand *clean* before a holy God. Not because we are clean, but because Jesus is clean.

To sin is human and to forgive is divine, and the divine act of the one and only God not only declares us clean, but makes us a new creation that is clean. When we have on the righteousness of Jesus, we look like Jesus.

"If we confess our sins, he is faithful and just to forgive us our sins and to cleanse us from all unrighteousness." **1 John 1:9 ESV**

Think about it. *Selah*

Day Thirty-four: Psalm 23:5

"You prepare a table before me in the presence of my enemies; you anoint my head with oil; my cup overflows."
Psalm 23:5 ESV

It is a fearful thing to be in the presence of those who are seeking to take your life. I have not been in the military, but my Dad and my brother have. My Dad was in World War II, and my brother was in Vietnam. My brother Dave told me that you really did not know who the enemy was and who your allies were. The person who cut your hair may be the one firing rockets into your camp the next day. That is a fear factor. My Dad was one of General Dwight D. Eisenhower's personal bodyguards during World War II, and they were prepared to deal with the enemy who might be embedded in England and France who may come by stealth with the aim of assassinating General Eisenhower. That was a fear factor, but to be under active gunfire and engaged with an aggressive enemy brings about great fear.

King David, the sweet Psalmist, relays quite a different situation concerning being in the presence of the enemy waiting for the battle. He says that the Lord prepared him for battle by setting up a feast, a banquet, or a good meal right where the enemy can see. What the enemy sees is the joy and laughter of friends eating together a meal that was prepared by the Good Shepherd himself. What the sheep were experiencing was peace, fulfillment, and comfort. Why? Because they were not the attack force, the Good Shepherd was. The dread of battle was not a concern because the Good Shepherd had everything under control and threw a banquet.

After the banquet God anoints our head with oil. What is that all about? Anointing with oil is to bring into remembrance a blessing that He has promised, or to confirm or publicly announce a blessing or a plan that He is to promise. Anointing with oil is a guarantee or seal of a promise. Anointing with oil is God putting to rest any doubt of His intentions for the one being anointed. This too is done in the presence of our enemies. They witness the anointing. This anointing brings great concern to the enemy and great peace to the one being anointed at the table of the Lord's feast.

We read in **Numbers 14:9** and **Romans 8:31** that we need not fear those who oppose us in doing that which God has given us to do because God is for us. If He is for us, then it really does not matter who or what is against us.

My conclusion to the *"you anoint my head with oil"* phrase is that goodness and mercy follow us all the days of our lives; goodness and mercy are in the very presence of battle of the enemy and on the battle ground itself. We should expect goodness and mercy from the Lord. Goodness is the grace that comes from the good hand of God. It is that peace we experience. We can expect it the rest of our lives. The mercy we experience involves those things that have been taken out of our lives by the good hand of God for our good and for His glory.

"You prepare a table before me in the presence of my enemies; you anoint my head with oil; my cup overflows." **Psalm 23:5 ESV**

Think about it. *Selah*

Day Thirty-five: James 1:2

"Count it all joy, my brothers, when you meet trials of various kinds." **James 1:2 ESV**

No one likes to be doubted. No on enjoys being questioned. We all would like to feel that others accept what we say as truth and take what we do with trust. The sad reality is that we are doubted, and we are often questioned in this life that we live; but it is best to understand that trust is something that is earned not granted. We earn respect and gain trust based totally upon the lives that we live before others and the experience or observation that others have of us.

Our concern in life ought not be whether we are left out or accepted by others, or whether we are doubted or accepted. Our concern should not be about the opposition we have in life. We should expect opposition. Our concern ought to be whether we are we doubting and resisting what God has said to us and are we faithfully doing what He has asked us to do. God is the fuel of our lives and the defense of our lives. We read in **Romans 8:31** that if God is for us, why should we worry about those who oppose us and resist us.

So, expect trials, expect times of testing in life, and expect God's intervention in our lives. Paul says in **Acts 20:24** that life is worth little unless I live it in doing what God has given me to do. As we are involved in doing what God has called us to do, we will experience trials. Jesus experienced doubting, opposition, and hatred in doing what the Father had sent Him to do, so we also ought to expect the same, **John 15:18–21.** Therefore, if we are expecting it, then we will count it complete joy when these times of testing and trials come.

"Count it all joy, my brothers, when you meet trials of various kinds," **James 1:2 ESV.** Trials have come in the lives of believers, and they will continue to come; but as they come, the believer should count it a pleasure to be questioned, doubted, and even tortured by the world. Remember, as we experience trials of all types, those who are involved in causing the trials and those who witness us *in* the trial are witnessing God's work in our lives. Trials do not mean failure; trials reflect dedication.

Think about it. *Selah*

Day Thirty-six: Psalm 1:6

"For the Lord knows the way of the righteous, but the way of the wicked will perish." **Psalm 1:6 ESV**

Did you know that God is complete power? Complete power leaves nothing out, and it lacks nothing. Complete power leaves nothing more to gain in power at any time from eternity past all the way into eternity future. God is not only complete power, but He also possesses complete knowledge. Complete knowledge leaves nothing left to learn. There was never a time that He did not possess complete knowledge. God did not *gain* knowledge. He *is* knowledge. Solomon, the wisest man who ever lived, wrote in **Proverbs 1:7** that the fear of the Lord is the beginning of our knowledge. Why? It is because God is the starting point of gaining knowledge and understanding.

God also has the ability to be everywhere at all times. This means that He not only *could be* everywhere at the same time but that He *is* everywhere at the same time. This means that He witnesses and observes everyone and everything from conception to completion with full knowledge, all at the same time. Not only that, but He planned it all. He is the Architect, the Inventor and the Creator of all things. It means he did not come up with the idea of all things, but He always had them in His mind because He is eternal, before beginning, and beyond the end.

God also never changes. Why should He need to change if He is complete? There is nothing about Him that can be added or improved upon in Himself. Now with this understanding of God, David says that the Lord knows the way of the righteous person, and He also knows well the way of the wicked person. God rewards the righteous person because of the righteousness of Jesus (**2 Corinthians 5:21**) and punishes the wicked person because of the deeds that he has done in his life.

John, the beloved disciple of Jesus, writes in **Revelation 20:11–15** about the Great White Throne Judgment and the Judgment Seat of Christ. The wicked were judged according to the things that they did in their lives, both good and bad, by the God who has complete knowledge and personal witness. All of their deeds were written in the "books." After their judgment by God, they were thrown into the eternal death fueled by the awesome, fearful, and extreme wrath of God. *"For we know him who said, 'Vengeance is mine; I will repay.' And again, 'The Lord will judge his people.' It is a fearful thing to fall into the hands of the living God."* **Hebrews 10:30 ESV**

"For the Lord knows the way of the righteous, but the way of the wicked will perish." **Psalm 1:6 ESV**

Think about it. *Selah*

Day Thirty-seven: Joshua 1:8

"This book of the law shall not depart from your mouth, but you shall meditate on it day and night, so that you may be careful to do according to all that is written in it. For then you will make your way prosperous, and then you will have good success."
Joshua 1:8 ESV

"Study to make yourself approved." Paul writes to Timothy in **2 Timothy 2:15** to study or to do your very best to be one that is approved by God as he expounds the Word of God to others. God wants His followers to know his Word, to understand what His Word means, and be able to apply his Word into our daily lives.

We can only do this by daily and continually being involved in reading His Word, meditating upon his Word, and listening to the Holy Spirit as He teaches us the application of His Word. It is only when we have that proper and good understanding of the written Word that we are able to help others.

Having a good and proper understanding of God's Word will guarantee that we will be prosperous in doing what God has given us to do. We will be a success in witnessing to others and profitable to the work of God in our lives.

Life is not about things on this earth but things in heaven. Jesus tells His disciples not to store up for themselves treasures on this earth but in heaven. Earth is temporary and heaven is eternal. Nothing rots, nothing rusts, and nothing decreases in heaven. In heaven, all things glow with the glory of God and are eternally profitable.

"This book of the law shall not depart from your mouth, but you shall meditate on it day and night, so that you may be careful to do according to all that is written in it. For then you will make your way prosperous, and then you will have good success."
Joshua 1:8 ESV

Think about it. *Selah*

Day Thirty-eight: Psalm 1:5

"Therefore the wicked will not stand in the judgment, or sinners in the congregation of the righteous."
Psalm 1:5 ESV

"You just don't stand a chance!" What is it about this statement that you do not understand? If you don't stand a chance, then you have no chance of seeing a different outcome. It means that you are helpless and without any hope. It means that no one really cares and no one is able to come to your defense, even if they wanted to do so.

What does David mean by the "wicked?" David is talking about those who are not good. The rich young ruler called Jesus "Good Teacher," and Jesus said there is none that is good, except God **(Mark 10:18)**. Only redeemed people are good, and they are not good because of the goodness in their lives but because of the goodness of God's righteousness upon their lives. So, the wicked are those who reject Jesus, those who reject His goodness and keep their wickedness. They are the wicked.

It is these people that stand in judgment before God. The fearful warning here is that even if they try to mask themselves by sitting in the congregation of the righteous, they are still exposed by the pure eyes of God. The association with the congregation of the righteous means you are comparing yourselves with their righteousness and that their righteousness is filthy rags, dirty diapers, and diseased, stinking wrappings of wounds. It is only the righteousness of Jesus that qualifies one to be a new creation.

Our association must be at the feet of Jesus, and that is the only escape. Otherwise, you don't stand a chance.

"Therefore the wicked will not stand in the judgment, nor sinners in the congregation of the righteous."
Psalm 1:5 ESV

Think about it. *Selah*

Day Thirty-nine: Psalm 1:4

"The wicked are not so, but are like the chaff that the wind drives away."
Psalm 1:4 ESV

Have you ever dropped a piece of paper and tried to pick it up, but the wind comes along and blows it just before you can get a grip on it? When that happens to me, it seems as though the wind is watching me and doesn't blow until I make a move toward the piece of paper. Sometimes the wind wins and blows the paper beyond me. It seems as though I can't figure out where the paper will go, and more often than not, it blows in the opposite direction that I anticipated.

David is talking about the husk of the wheat seed here in **Psalm 1:4**. The chaff goes in all directions, up down and all around. It is impossible to predict. This is the way it is with the wicked or those who reject the saving power of God. They have no real purpose or direction in life and cannot be depended upon. They are not really sure of their own future. Though there are some who may be working toward a specific and self-determined goal, it cannot be depended upon. They are left to the whims of the time and the actions of others. They are "lost." They are the reason Jesus came, but they are driven away from Him. Unless they respond to the voice of Jesus, who made all things, they have no hope.

Are you driven by the winds of the day? Does it seem that you have been carried far beyond where you planned and hoped to be? There is an answer, and that answer is Jesus, the one whom the winds, the waves, and the storms must obey.

It could be that you are a believer but have been caught up in the winds. Draw near to Jesus, and He will draw near to you. Cast your eyes upon Him because He cares for you. Listen to His voice and obey, and He will give you direction and supply what you need.

Come to Jesus who gives us peace. Reach out to Jesus whose hand is reaching down to you. Take hold of His hand, and you will never be the same again. You will be safe in His arms.

"The wicked are not so, but are like the chaff that the wind drives away."
Psalm 1:4 ESV

Think about it. *Selah*

Day Forty: Jeremiah 29:11

"For I know the plans I have for you, declares the Lord, plans for welfare and not for evil, to give you a future and a hope." **Jeremiah 29:11 ESV**

Many a Christian young person has taken this verse as their life's verse. The future often seems dark but is hoped to be bright. Parents of every generation have been fearful for their children. They know how it was when they were where their children are, and they see how the world has deteriorated. Things today, they say, are far worse than they were when I was their age.

But the youth of today see brightness and are optimistic about their future because of a hope that is within them, the same hope that was within us when we were their age. But there is a difference between the youth in Christ and the youth outside of Christ. Those outside of Christ place their hope in *a good chance* or perhaps *good luck*; but those in Christ have a **faith**, which is a hope that does not fail because it is totally based upon Him.

Jesus is the master designer, the arranger, and the perfecter of our faith. That faith and that hope rest totally upon Him who desires that we succeed and provides what is needed to succeed. This desire for success will come in opposition to the evil that will be thrown before us, and all those evil things will be used for our good **(Genesis 50:20)**. God will weave everything in our lives together to make a beautiful tapestry that will bring glory to Him and will be good for us **(Romans 8:29)**. God will bring before every temptation that we may experience a way of escape **(1**

Corinthians 10:13). God will supply and make available to us way beyond what we need according to His riches in heaven through Christ Jesus (**Philippians 4:19**). His working in our lives will bring about things that are beyond our wildest dream (**Ephesians 3:20**).

This is what God has for our future. The conditions of this world cannot hinder His will for us in the slightest degree. Having said that, remember that all things that happen are not good, but God uses all things that happen to us for good.

Well, the future is good if your eternity is good. God has good plans for us. They are divine plans and they are great plans. They are plans for a profitable and good future and a hope that will not fail.

"For I know the plans I have for you, declares the Lord, plans for welfare and not for evil, to give you a future and a hope." **Jeremiah 29:11 ESV**

Think about it. *Selah*

Day Forty- one: 2 Timothy 3:17

"That the man of God may be complete, equipped for every good work."
2 Timothy 3:17 ESV

Competent is being complete. The dictionary gives a definition of being able to answer all requirements. Someone who is competent is a person of responsibility, a person of means, and who is dependable. He can be relied upon and dispels any cause of worry or fretting. A competent person carries with him comfort, peace, and confidence and leaves comfort, peace, and confidence with those to whom that person is responsible.

When something needs to be done, it is the competent person who will complete the task and complete it with excellence and expediency. If a person is in need of advice, he will seek out a person of competence. The Psalmist tells us that the Lord is our rock, our helper, our fortress, our deliverer, our shelter, our help, our hope and many other words that carry the feeling of competence.

This is what Paul is telling Timothy, and it is what God desires for us to achieve. He desires for us to study, to spend time to know the Word of God, and to be able to relay the Word of God with accurate understanding and reliable counsel. The Holy Spirit is our teacher and guide in acquiring this competent understanding of God's Word, as we become a scholar of God's Word.

A. W. Tozer writes: *"The task of a scholar is to guarantee the purity of the text, to get as close as possible to the Word as originally given. He may compare Scripture with Scripture until he discovers the true meaning of the text, but right there his authority ends. He must never sit in judgment upon what is written. He must not bring the meaning of the Word before the bar of reason."* This gives real competence to the scholar of God's Word. This equips him with the authority and adds competence to what he says and teaches. The man of God is now relaying what God says and not what he thinks or what some author has written.

"That the man of God may be complete, equipped for every good work."
2 Timothy 3:17 ESV

When we seek God, He will equip us with a good understanding and all the provisions that are needed to competently complete what He has called us to do. We can depend upon Him for He is competent.

Think about it. *Selah*

Day Forty-two: James 1:3

"For you know that the testing of your faith produces steadfastness." **James 1:3 ESV**

Have you ever been challenged? I know you have been because anyone who achieves any goal has had to overcome challenges to get to that goal. It takes effort, it takes determination, and it takes "stick-to-itiveness." To be challenged is to be tested.

Before I make a purchase of something of value, often I will consult *Consumer Reports* and check what they have written about that item. *Consumer Reports* is an organization composed of scientists, engineers, and technicians who spend time, money, and effort to test things and rate them as to their dependability, effectiveness, and efficiency and write a report concerning their findings. If that item passes their testing, I know it is reliable, dependable, and will be steadfast in the performing of its purpose.

James tells us to have the proper understanding of testing. It is the times of testing in our lives with the challenges to our efforts and development as messengers of Christ that bring about our steadfastness, our durability, our dependability, and our competency. Testing brings confidence. It makes us durable, capable, and sufficient to the task before us. We need to know this in order not to be discouraged by testing.

"For you know that the testing of your faith produces steadfastness." **James 1:3 ESV**

Think about it. Selah

Day Forty-three: Acts 20:24

"But I do not account my life of any value nor as precious to myself, if only I may finish my course and the ministry that I received from the Lord Jesus, to testify to the gospel of the grace of God." **Acts 20:24 ESV**

This verse is one of my life verses. At the time of this writing I am 68 years of age. In 2013 my wife, Bobbie, and I retired and are presently retooling, adjusting, and changing lanes in our ministry. Bobbie retired from teaching in public schools and I retired from being in full time Gospel Ministry for 43 years. Of those 43 years, I have been a Youth Pastor, a Minister of Music, a Christian school teacher, and a Pastoral Care Pastor. Since retirement, I have been involved in pulpit supply and worship pastor supply. I have also begun to do some writing as I seek to be a source of encouragement and teaching by bringing the light of God's Word to other Christians as well as to those who may not know Jesus Christ, God's only begotten son and redeemer of mankind.

My sole desire in life is to be used of God in doing what He calls me to do. Nothing that I have done in life really amounts to anything except that which God has used me to do in the lives of others. I used the word *retired,* but that does not mean that I have quit. I have only just begun a new segment in my life. As I mentioned earlier, I have just changed lanes in the road of life.

My aim is to cause others to see Jesus more clearly, to depend upon Him more fully, and to follow Him more closely in what He may call them to do. I want to dispel discouragement with encouragement and to build up those who have been beaten down by other Christians. I want to hold the hands of those younger than I who have begun their battle with the principalities and powers around them and the forces of evil that are readily at work in their young lives. I want to help them see the strength that is found in Christ and to acknowledge the fact that it is their very weakness that God will use to bring about victory.

Yes, life is worth little unless I use it to do that which God has called me to do. Don't seek any other goal; don't hold on to the gloss of life. Look full into the glory of Jesus, depend upon the grace and mercy that is sufficient for your struggle, and use your life to do what God has called you to do.

"But I do not account my life of any value nor as precious to myself, if only I may finish my course and the ministry that I received from the Lord Jesus, to testify to the gospel of the grace of God." **Acts 20:24 ESV**

Think about it. *Selah*

Day Forty-four: Hebrews 4:12

"For the word of God is living and active, sharper than any two-edged sword, piercing to the division of soul and of spirit, of joints and of marrow, and discerning the thoughts and intentions of the heart." **Hebrews 4:12 ESV**

God's Word is something that the believer in Christ Jesus must have at his disposal. It is by God's Word, or Scripture, that we receive power to live a victorious life in Christ Jesus. The **New Living Translation** begins **Hebrews 4:12** with *"For the word of God is alive and powerful."* We defeat Satan's power in our life by the Word of God. Satan misuses God's Word. He abuses and distorts God's Word to anyone who may listen to him. Satan even tried to misuse, abuse, and distort God's Word with Jesus as he tempted him in the wilderness. In **Luke 4,** Jesus demonstrated for us how to be victorious over Satan by having a sharp, living, and active understanding of God's Word. Even today we encounter the distortion of God's Word by those outside of the family of God.

The believer must spend time in God's Word under the influence of Holy Spirit in order to have a proper, clear, and genuine understanding of God's Word. The person who writes the letter is the one who can apply that letter in the way it was written, and the third person of the Trinity, the Holy Spirit, is the personality sent by Jesus to do just that. Do not depend on theologians, scientists, educators, politicians, and individuals of influence to lead your understanding. They will lead you down a wrong path. It may seem right, but it leads to destruction.

God's Word interprets God's Word. *"For the word of God is living and active, sharper than any two-edged sword, piercing to the division of soul and of spirit, of joints and of marrow, and discerning the thoughts and intentions of the heart,"* **Hebrews 4:12 ESV.** God's Word gives us the understanding of life, it guides us in making right decisions, and it cleans our thought life. God minds our thoughts and corrects our intentions when they are disingenuous.

God's Word is the tool needed for a good life. It is God's Word that will shape a nation to become a godly nation that will be the good hand of God to godless nations. God's word can heal a nation, and it can heal a marriage. It heals broken fellowship, it exposes evil, and it highlights good. *"For the word of God is alive and powerful."* **(Hebrews 4:12)**

Think about it. *Selah*

Day Forty-five: Romans 8:1

"There is therefore now no condemnation for those who are in Christ Jesus."
Romans 8:1 ESV

To be condemned is to be of no value. It is to be disapproved, and it is to be criticized, denounced, reviled, berated, rebuked, and reproved. A person who is condemned is labeled as totally unacceptable, unwanted and is censured and sent away.

We want to be accepted by others and not condemned. We want to be approved, not rejected, and sought out, not shunned. We want to be desired by others rather than rejected by others. Paul gives some good news here in **Romans 8:1**. The *Good News* is that in Christ Jesus there is no condemnation at all. Condemnation is found outside of Christ Jesus. People will condemn but if you are in Christ Jesus, He does not condemn you because you are His and in His care. Jesus does not condemn those for whom He died. He gives them life, and He gives them joy, peace, love, and approval.

The opinions of people do not matter, but the opinion of Jesus does. Paul writes in **2 Corinthians 5:21** that the Father made His sinless Son Jesus to be sin and made us to be the righteousness of Jesus. This is not condemnation; it is mercy. It is acceptance, and it is the reason that those who are in Christ Jesus can go to heaven. They are new creations in Christ Jesus and completely acceptable to God.

If you have accepted God's Son as your Savior, the Father accepts you. If you reject His Son, He rejects and condemns you. In **John 3:17-18** we read, *"For God did not send His Son into the world to condemn the world, but that the world through Him might be saved. He who believes in Him is not condemned; but he who does not believe is condemned already, because he has not believed in the name of the only begotten Son of God."* **(NKJV)**

What a glorious promise! *"There is therefore now no condemnation for those who are in Christ Jesus."* **Romans 8:1 ESV**

What is there to condemn when you have the righteousness of Jesus?

Think about it. *Selah*

Day Forty-six: John 3:17

"For God did not send his Son into the world to condemn the world, but in order that the world might be saved through him." **John 3:17 ESV**

If God is love and He came into the world to save people, how can a loving God send anyone to hell? Have you ever heard that? I'm sure you have, and it is usually used as a reason to refute the idea that there is a God. The problem here is a misunderstanding of God's Word or an aggressive attack upon believers to discredit and disprove the Bible and the existence of God.

Yes, God is love and yes He came to redeem mankind, but the Bible does not say that God sends anyone to hell. It proclaims just the opposite. God came to save people from hell, not to condemn people to hell. The truth is that people were already condemned to hell, and so Jesus came to reclaim, redeem, and to snatch people from hell.

Ravi Zacharias has said it this way: *"God did not send his only Son into the world to make bad people good but to make dead people alive. He did not come to make poor people rich, for our treasures are in heaven. He did not come to make sick people healthy temporarily, but to give new life, eternal life. He didn't come to make our lives free from trouble. He is peace, real peace in the time of trouble. He didn't come to make us famous but to point us to the Famous One, Jesus."*

So you see, God does love you, and He wants you to love Him. *"For God did not send his Son into the world to condemn the world, but in order that the world might be saved through him."* **John 3:17 ESV** Think about it. *Selah*

Day Forty-seven: Hebrews 11:1

"Now faith is the assurance of things hoped for, the conviction of things not seen." **Hebrews 11:1 ESV**

Christianity is not a religion. It is a Faith. Christianity is seen in a life lived in hope or in a holy expectation of the fulfillment of what Jesus taught about who He was, why He came, and what He will do. Christianity is seen in a person who responds by faith to the Good News of Jesus, and who lives his life of faith in the promises of Jesus as he carries that Good News to others.

This faith that we have is our assurance of our future. It alone is our hope and the foundation for the convictions that we have and the life that we live. It is how others can visibly see that which cannot be seen.

The Holy Spirit is the spiritual glasses that we wear which enable us to see clearly and understand completely God's Word to us and His will for us. Our faith guides us, leads us, protects us, strengthens us, and sustains us.

"Now faith is the assurance of things hoped for, the conviction of things not seen."
Hebrews 11:1 ESV

Think about it. *Selah*

Day Forty-eight: James 1:4

"And let steadfastness have its full effect, that you may be perfect and complete, lacking in nothing." **James 1:4 ESV**

The *sayings* go, "Nobody's perfect" and "You can't have everything." These are not just *sayings*; they are true. No one is perfect. Jesus reminded the rich young ruler in **Luke 18:18** that there is only one who is good. You can't have everything, but here in James we now read that we can be perfect, and we can have everything.

As far as humanity is concerned, there is none righteous, and there is no one who is good, profitable, or trustworthy. The only way any created human beings could be perfect, complete, and trustworthy in themselves is for them to be recreated, made new, or to have a start-over. That is exactly what God does with the believer in Christ Jesus. We are "new creations," created in Christ Jesus. *"Therefore, if anyone is in Christ, he is a new creation. The old has passed away; behold, the new has come,"* **2 Corinthians 5:17 ESV.**

The new creation part is all God's doing and our part, while here on this earth, is to be steadfast, to be faithful, and to press on toward the prize or mark (**Philippians 3:14**). When we are steadfast as we work out our salvation, we display before others the power of Christ Jesus, and we come to the realization that we are perfect after all and there is nothing lacking in our mission of spreading the Good News (**Philippians 1:6; 4:13 & 19**).

"And let steadfastness have its full effect, that you may be perfect and complete, lacking in nothing." **James 1:4 ESV**

Think about it. *Selah*

Day Forty-nine: James 1:5

"If any of you lacks wisdom, let him ask God, who gives generously to all without reproach, and it will be given him." **James 1:5 ESV**

Decisions, decisions, decisions. Life is filled with decisions. Most are easy, but there are many that are very difficult, and it is those decisions that bring stress to our lives. Actually, all decision-making should not be made without thought. Many of those decisions we might think at the time to be small, turn out to be life-changing decisions. Who should be on your friend list? Should I go to that party? Should I take that smoke, take that drink, or take that ride? We may use as our deciding factor, "everybody else is doing it" or "it's not that bad," only to come to the shocking revelation that everybody else was wrong and it actually was a bad thing after all. Decisions require wisdom, real wisdom, and reliable wisdom. Who gives that wisdom?

James tells us if we need wisdom, then we ought to ask God. Solomon says much about wisdom. In the first chapter of Proverbs, verse 7, he says that the fear of the Lord is the very beginning of knowledge. In other words, a good understanding of God is where wisdom begins. If we know God, we have what is necessary to gain understanding and receive wisdom in life. God made everything and He knows everything; therefore, where else should we go for wisdom? He knows all things.

If we know God, we need to also know that He loves us, He gave His Son for us, He redeemed us, and He wants to supply all our needs and provide strength, peace, and understanding in our lives. With that understanding, we can come to the conclusion that if we need anything, we can go to Him with boldness and assurance that if we ask anything of Him, He hears us. Therefore, if you need wisdom, ask God for that wisdom. Do not doubt Him, because He does not show favoritism. He shows love. If you ask Him for wisdom, He will give you the wisdom you asked for and wisdom beyond what you asked.

"If any of you lacks wisdom, let him ask God, who gives generously to all without reproach, and it will be given him." **James 1:5 ESV**

Think About it. *Selah*

Day Fifty: John 1:2

"He was in the beginning with God." **John 1:2 ESV**

Jesus is the only begotten Son of God. He is the undisputable Son of God, and He *is* God. When reading the book of **Genesis**, we read the pronouns *us* and *our*. As John, the beloved disciple of Jesus begins his Gospel, he wants the reader to have a clear understanding of who he is writing about. He tells us that Jesus is the Word. He is the Word for He is the *voice* of the Father. At creation God "said" let there be, and there was. Creation exploded and quickly responded to the *voice*, the Word.

It was this Jesus that John is writing about that was with God before the beginning.   Before there was anything, there was God, and Jesus was there also.

This is the God who became a man and experienced the same temptations, difficulties, and pulls of Satan that man experienced. He conquered that sin and the grave to rise victorious. **1 Corinthians 15:55**

"He was in the beginning with God." **John 1:2 ESV**

Think about it. *Selah*

Day Fifty-one: Matthew 5:16

"In the same way, let your light shine before others, so that they may see your good works and give glory to your Father who is in heaven." **Matthew 5:16 ESV**

Jesus had just revealed His heart to His disciples and those who were listening that day on the mountain. He opened His heart and shed light upon what their purpose in following Him should be. He preserved in their hearts that their eternal life with Him in heaven, not this earth, is the major objective. He wanted them to see that there was a benefit in following Him in that with the struggle of living a life in Christ, there were blessings associated with the struggle. He wanted them to see that a life lived for Him was well worth the struggle, the persecution, and the opposition.

Here in verse sixteen of chapter five of Matthew, Jesus encourages His followers to strive to faithfully live that life before others so that they would be a light, an inspiration, and a preservative to those who witness their faithfulness and their determination. In turn, they would see how God blesses them for their faithfulness. Their observation would be a witness to them and give the followers of Jesus the opportunity to present the Good News to them. The observers would give glory to God for His faithfulness in the lives of his followers.

Letting your light shine, allowing God to glow to the world, is a wonderful way that anyone can be an effective witness for Christ Jesus. Don't hide your life. Let it shine before men so that they may give glory and honor to our good and great Father who is in heaven.

"In the same way, let your light shine before others, so that they may see your good works and give glory to your Father who is in heaven." **Matthew 5:16 ESV**

Think about it. *Selah*

Day Fifty-two: Matthew 5:3

"Blessed are the poor in spirit, for theirs is the kingdom of heaven." **Matthew 5:3 ESV**

Who are the poor in spirit? The poor in spirit are those of us who are downcast in spirit. They are those of us who feel defeated, unloved, taken advantage of, and suffer feelings of helplessness and no worth. They are people who know they need help but feel that no one really cares. Those are the people that Jesus is referring to in **Matthew 5:3**.

I would say all of us have experienced those feelings from time to time and many live their lives controlled by those hindrances. A defeated life is by definition a life lived void of victory, conquest, and strength. Jesus says to those people that you are blessed because you have a helper, you have a Savior, and you have a sure defense, a conqueror, and a victorious deliverer. That person is Jesus Christ who is for you, and if He is for you, who is it that can be against you? He is Lord over all. He is the judge, avenger, and power over all. This is the person who disperses blessings and extends to you the right to live with Him in the eternal Kingdom of Heaven.

Therefore, Jesus has the authority to say, "You are of all people most blessed. Trust me, be happy, joyful, and feel loved for I have reserved for you the Kingdom of Heaven."

"Blessed are the poor in spirit, for theirs is the kingdom of heaven." **Matthew 5:3 ESV**

Think about it. *Selah*

Day Fifty-three: Deuteronomy 6:5

"You shall love the Lord your God with all your heart and with all your soul and with all your might."
Deuteronomy 6:5 ESV

A great athlete gives a hundred and ten percent. He or she goes above and beyond to stretch themselves beyond their natural tendencies. They give all and the reward is greatness along with the victor's crown. To be great in anything will require going the extra mile to achieve the goal. Winning is the important thing and losing is not an option. Giving all means that what you do is done with all your heart. You struggle with all your being. It means that you leave nothing in reserve. Everything is drained down to empty. It is "peddle-to-the-metal" all the way as you go all out to win.

The goal of the believer is to do what God has given him to do and to have no other ambition in life but to complete that mission.   Bobby Richardson, the star second baseman of the New York Yankees during the late Fifties and early Sixties, was nominated for MVP in the American League nine times. He won five gold gloves, played in 7 all-Star games, and won the MVP of the World Series although his team did not win that series. He said, *"God's will, nothing more, nothing less and nothing else."* Missionary Jim Elliot wrote: *"He is no fool who gives what he cannot keep to gain that which he cannot lose"* and *"Wherever you are, be all there."* He also wrote: *"Live it to the hilt in every situation you believe to be the will of God."* This is living a loving life, living it with all your heart, living it with all your soul, and living it with all your might.

"You shall love the Lord your God with all your heart and with all your soul and with all your might."
Deuteronomy 6:5 ESV

So, what about your life?

Think about it. *Selah*

Day Fifty-four: Ephesians 2:10

"For we are his workmanship, created in Christ Jesus for good works, which God prepared beforehand that we should walk in them." **Ephesians 2:10 ESV**

A skilled craftsman's work is admired and sought out. In the building of the temple, Solomon employed and assigned the work and skill of the best craftsman for their area to create specific items of the Temple in Jerusalem. In **1 Kings 7:13-14** we read: *"And King Solomon sent and brought Hiram from Tyre. He was the son of a widow of the tribe of Naphtali, and his father was a man of Tyre, a worker in bronze.   And he was full of wisdom, understanding, and skill for making any work in bronze. He came to King Solomon and did all his work."* **ESV**

Solomon used only the best to create the best to be used in the Temple of God in Jerusalem. Anything that would be used in worship in the Temple that was less than the best was simply undesirable and unacceptable. The same is true for us today when we worship God. We should seek the best that we have or can get.

Paul tells us that it is the skill of God or His workmanship that is needed to create something that is acceptable. It is His good work that He prepared before our conversion to make us acceptable, profitable and holy enough to be used by Him. He expects us to walk in a manner worthy of His workmanship in our daily lives. We were created for good works, not shady works or bad works, but His work, His workmanship.   If we do anything less, it is dishonoring to His workmanship and to Himself. You don't display a Rembrandt in your bathroom. You display it in a manner that is honoring to the painter, the creator, the skilled painter, and the workman. You need to prepare a good place for it. Not just any place will do.

So, we need to let our light shine before others so they can see our good works and God's workmanship and glorify the Creator in heaven, **Matthew 5:16.**

"For we are his workmanship, created in Christ Jesus for good works, which God prepared beforehand that we should walk in them." **Ephesians 2:10 ESV**

Think about it. Selah

Day Fifty-five: Romans 10:9

"Because, if you confess with your mouth that Jesus is Lord and believe in your heart that God raised him from the dead, you will be saved." **Romans 10:9 ESV**

Do you like to hear absolutes? They say that there are no absolutes. But there are things that are absolutely true. There are not many of them, but there are absolutes. If it is absolutely true, there is no doubt about that absolute. You can trust an absolute. There is no place for doubt with an absolute; and your life can be securely built upon an absolute.

Paul states an absolute in **Romans 10:9**; and that is, if you confess with your mouth, if you admit verbally and audibly that Jesus Christ is God's Son, and with a pure heart believe it, you will be saved, period. It involves nothing more, nothing less than admitting you are a sinner and that you are helpless on your own to achieve forgiveness of sin, and you will be saved.

That, my friend, is an absolute. That statement can be totally relied upon; you can take it to heaven's bank. I heard **Mark Bearden** say in a Refresh Conference at Sherwood Baptist Church in Albany, Georgia, *"You don't need to get your act together in order to come to Jesus for forgiveness of sin. The only way you can get your act together is to come to Jesus Christ and let the Holy Spirit work in your life to get your act together."* Jesus is the only way. He is your only hope, and that is an absolute.

Did you know that this absolute is something that God planned? (**Ephesians 2:4-10**) Do you understand that aside from this plan, there is no other plan? (**Acts 4:12**)

"Because, if you confess with your mouth that Jesus is Lord and believe in your heart that God raised him from the dead, you will be saved." **Romans 10:9 ESV**

Have you made this confession? If not, you are without hope. The good news is, although you are without hope, there is a hope that does not disappoint and that hope comes by confessing with your mouth and sincerely believing with all of your heart that Jesus Christ is Lord. Why would you doubt that? It is the major absolute in life that brings eternal life.

Think about it. *Selah*

Day Fifty-six: Matthew 5:6

"Blessed are those who hunger and thirst for righteousness, for they shall be satisfied."
Matthew 5:6 ESV

There is nothing like a cool glass of cold water when you are thirsty. The pure satisfaction of that cold glass of water quenching the thirst that you had can be well described in the words of the Alka-Seltzer commercial of the late Sixties and Seventies: *"Plop, plop, fizz, fizz, oh, what a relief it is."* It is a welcomed satisfaction.

I remember going to North Korea with the Son's of Jubal, a group of ministers of music, church music leaders, and pastors from Georgia. The experience itself was an act of God; because we went there at North Korea's invitation, and they allowed us to sing our songs of the faith because we sang some of their songs in Korean. My point here is concerning hunger. The food which we had was, to say the least, *different*, and after sixteen days of being there and in China, I hungered for familiar food. I remember after landing in Atlanta, Georgia, my son Justin and I went to a local restaurant and ordered a steak. That was the most enjoyable and satisfying meal I think I can ever remember eating before or since. What a blessed event that was.

In **Matthew 5:6**, Jesus relates to the crowd that day and to us today that the reward, the blessing from heaven for His followers who have a great thirst in need of quenching and a great hunger for living the righteous life of Christ, is to have the righteousness of Christ adorned upon them and displayed in their lives, whereby they will experience divine satisfaction in their lives. The difficulties that we may experience and the opposition we may face will be relieved and overcome by the pure satisfaction from our quest to live righteously. We have no other desire; we crave no other thing other than the righteousness of Jesus. We have been *"made"* the righteousness of Jesus by the Father, as we read in **2 Corinthians 5:21**.

"Blessed are those who hunger and thirst for righteousness, for they shall be satisfied." **Matthew 5:6 ESV**

Have you experienced the feeling of satisfaction having determined to develop a life of righteousness? Do you have that hunger within you? Is your mouth dry and in need of the pure, cool water from the cup of God? *"Oh, what a relief it is!"*

Think about it. *Selah*

Day Fifty-seven: Exodus 14:14

"The Lord will fight for you, and you have only to be silent." **Exodus 14:14 ESV**

Bullies understand strength and they cower from it. A bully looks for those who are weak and unleashes his fury upon them. A bully needs to be around the weak to feel powerful and important. Fear is how he achieves his goal. Fear is what a bully wants to instill. Insecurity is what he fears most. It is at the root of his quest in life. A bully can be a boy or a girl, a man or a woman, a community, a people, or a nation. Bullies are sprinkled all throughout our lives. We have seen them, and we know them personally. Some people conquer them while others continue to be enslaved by them.

The children of Israel were bullied by the nation of Egypt and more specifically by Pharaoh. They could only do what he allowed them to do. They were supposed to be following God and worshiping Him, but Pharaoh would not allow it. God sent Moses as His ambassador to deliver Israel and to announce to Pharaoh that his bullying days had come to an end.

God did not require Israel to fight because He would fight for them. They had no requirement other than to be silent, to stand still, and to watch God. The bully that had been a part of their daily lives and was advancing upon them would be gone on this day, and they would not see him anymore, **Exodus 14:13.**

If God is our strength, if He is for us, if He is against those who might rise up against us, what is there to fear

(**Romans 8:31**)? We just need to be silent, be still, and know that He is God. There is peace in knowing that God will fight for us. This brings a holy hush upon us, but it is a fearful thing for those who stand before an angry God. **Hebrews 10:31**

"The Lord will fight for you and you have only to be silent." **Exodus 14:14 ESV**

Think about it. *Selah*

Day Fifty-eight: Matthew 5:4

"Blessed are those who mourn, for they shall be comforted." **Matthew 5:4 ESV**

To mourn is to feel deep sorrow, grief, or regret for the loss or disappearance of someone dear. A person who is mourning needs the comfort, compassion, and consolation of others. Comfort, on the other hand, is being in a state of ease and unrestrained peace and having freedom from feelings of grief.

Friends are those who can bring comfort by the compassion that they display and the consolation that is evidenced by their mere presence. It is good to have friends. There are those we may call friends but who cannot be counted upon. We read in **Proverbs 18:24**, however, that there is a friend who sticks with you through it all. This is a real friend, and all others are mere acquaintances.

Jesus calls us friends, not servants or mere acquaintances (**John 15:15**). We can confide in Him, we can tell Him all our fears, all our troubles, all our concerns in life, and much more. He listens to us, He hears us, and He is present with us in those times of sorrow, grief, loss, and regret. His presence brings peace, and it brings comfort delivered with a loving touch.

Yes, *"Blessed are those who mourn, for they shall be comforted,"* **Matthew 5:4 ESV.** For we have the very greatest of all comforters with us. If we look up the word *comforter*, we see the Holy Spirit, the third person of the Trinity. He is God with us. We have with us a friend and a comfort, one who dispels fear, and disperses comfort.

Day Fifty-nine: Matthew 5:5

"Blessed are the meek, for they shall inherit the earth."
Matthew 5:5 ESV

A meek person is not a weak person. A meek person is one who has power but it is withheld in mercy. A meek person is a caring person, a kind person, and loving person. To be meek is to have an attribute of Jesus, for He is meek and mild.

Jesus tells us in **Matthew 5:5** that those who are meek are heirs of the earth, the new earth that He will one day create after this present earth is destroyed. This new earth will be our inheritance, our dwelling place, **Revelation 21**.

"Blessed are the meek, for they shall inherit the earth." Satan is the prince and the power of this present earth, but he is no king. His place of power will suddenly be destroyed and he knows it. But, those meek ones, those followers of Christ, are the heirs of the new earth, and it is a promised possession. It is a secure possession, and it is an eternal possession.

Don't live your life trying to get all you can and *"can"* all you can get because this life on earth is temporary. Don't strive for possessions and power on this present earth because they will not last or satisfy. Follow the example of Christ Jesus who while on this earth lived a poor, meek, and unappreciated life only to sit down beside the Father and at His throne where one day every knee will bow. Every voice will one day proclaim that He is indeed Lord of Lords and King of Kings.

"Blessed are the meek, for they shall inherit the earth."
Matthew 5:5 ESV

Think about it. *Selah*

Day Sixty: Matthew 5:7

"Blessed are the merciful, for they shall receive mercy."
Matthew 5:7 ESV

"I fall upon the mercy of the court, your honor." Why would a person say that? A person who falls upon the mercy of the court has no defense. He has no excuse and no other option but to hope that the court will not give him what he knows that he deserves.

Mercy is not giving a person that which he deserves. A person seeking mercy does not want justice for justice is giving him what he actually deserves. Justice shows no mercy. Every person ever born on this earth is born into sin. They are born guilty before God and every person born on this earth deserves the wrath of God. **Hebrews 10:31** refers to the awesome fear that overtakes a person who stands guilty before an all-powerful, all knowing, ever present, and unchanging God. The only chance anyone has is the mercy of God, and it is promised only to those who believe in the only begotten Son of God, confess that they are unworthy having no power of their own, and ask for forgiveness from the only one who can forgive. *"To sin is human, to forgive is divine,"* the poet Alexander Pope wrote.

Jesus proclaims that when we are merciful to others, when we choose not to act in justice and but choose to be merciful instead, it gives glory to God, and He disperses mercy to us in turn. God loves mercy, and we, too, ought to love mercy. It is so easy, so natural, and so legal to want others to get what they deserve. It is so easy to pray that others will get what they deserve and forget that we are not getting what we deserve. We are getting mercy.

So, my challenge to you and to myself is to be a merciful follower of Christ and to be a reflection of Him, not the opposite.

"Blessed are the merciful, for they shall receive mercy."
Matthew 5:7 ESV

Think about it. *Selah*

Day Sixty-one: Matthew 5:8

"Blessed are the pure in heart, for they shall see God."
Matthew 5:8 ESV

In order to stand before a holy God, one must be holy. In order to be in the presence of a righteous God, one must in turn be righteous. How on earth can we sinful human beings stand in the presence of a holy, righteous God? The answer to that question is we cannot for we are earthly, and there is nothing on earth that can change us from the sinful, unrighteous and filthy rags that we are. It would have to take an act of heaven, not an act of this sinful earth, to make the change. It would take a new creation act. We can't be cleaned up. We must be made over. This is exactly what God did. God makes the believer a new creation. We are new creations, **2 Corinthians 5:21**.

The believer is not pure because of our deeds and actions, but we have been made pure because we have been made the righteousness of Jesus. We often call this being born again. In order to be on this earth, one must be born physically. In order to be in heaven, one must be born again or born spiritually. Jesus explained this to Nicodemus in **John 3**.

What a blessed thought that I can be made pure! *"Blessed are the pure in heart, for they shall see God,"* **Matthew 5:8 ESV**. What a blessed thought that I one day will stand confidently and rightfully before God! It is all because of the righteousness of Jesus.

Think about it. *Selah*

Day Sixty-two: Genesis 1:2

"The earth was without form and void, and darkness was over the face of the deep. And the Spirit of God was hovering over the face of the waters." **Genesis 1:2 ESV**

Without form, nothing, void, without worth; covered with darkness or clothed in darkness and in need of light, purpose, worth and substance. A hopeless situation is a situation void of the touch of God. Where darkness is, God is not there and where God is, darkness cannot be. The characteristics of darkness are insecurity, fear, and the threat of impending destruction. Before the creation of the earth and the universe, there was nothing, but when the Spirit of God, or the Holy Spirit, began to move, things began to change for the good for God is good.

This is the situation of the life that is void of God. It is there that one will find questions about the future. It is there that one finds the presence of fear, insecurity, and threat. These things change when the presence of God is injected to that life. Where there is God, there is liberty, there is peace, there is direction, there is hope, faith, love, purpose, worth and support. Where God is, there is a future, there is security and provision, and there is love.

Don't live your life outside of God. If you have received Jesus Christ as your Savior and as your Lord, or your provider and guide, then you have a secure future. You can rest in the promise of his Word.

Genesis begins with **nothing**: *"The earth was without form and void, and darkness was over the face of the deep. And the Spirit of God was hovering over the face of the waters,"* **Genesis 1:2 ESV.** But when God is added, there we find **something**. You are something and you have worth, so much worth that the Father sent His only begotten Son in to this worthless world just for you and in order that you would discover your worth, your eternal worth.

Think about it. *Selah*

Day Sixty-three: John 15:7

"If you abide in me, and my words abide in you, ask whatever you wish, and it will be done for you."
John 15:7 ESV
"Ask whatever you wish, and it will be done for you."
John 15:7 ESV
"Ye have not because ye ask not." **James 4:2 KJV**
"If you ask me anything in my name, I will do it."
John 14:14 ESV

These are promises and those verses can be counted upon. They can be relied upon, but they are verses that are also misunderstood because there is a caveat or a condition that goes along with them.

God does promise to supply all our physical and social needs. He does promise to be our provision in all things for the needs that we have, but for the requests that we make, He acts as a loving Father. Some are withheld and some are delayed, but all are done for our well-being and protection. At times we ask amiss or for things to be used for our own misguided ambitions (**James 4:2**).

God is in control of everything. Nothing can deter God's will nor can it alter His will. His will for us is that we obey His Word and that we carry his Good News to all we meet. His will is for us to be good ambassadors, good stewards, and a reflection of Him to all who may cross our paths in life.

So, what am I saying? I am saying that our major drive in life should be to glorify God as Jesus glorified Him. I am saying that we must abide in Christ as He abode in the Father. If we do that, then our aim in life would not be to glorify ourselves, and we would not ask for things that hinder us from serving Christ. If we live such a life, then anything that we ask will be pleasing to the Father, pleasing to the Son, and pleasing to the Holy Spirit, and they will lavish upon us things that exceed our ability to ask (**Ephesians 3:20**).

"If you abide in me, and my words abide in you, ask whatever you wish, and it will be done for you." **John 15:7 ESV**

Think about it. *Selah*

Day Sixty-four: Galatians 5:16

"But I say, walk in the Spirit, and you will not gratify the desires of the flesh."
Galatians 5:16 ESV

To live a life that is pleasing to God is the desire of all believers; yet it is not something that is simple to do. The believers in Jesus Christ live *in* this world but they are not *of* this world because heaven is our home. We are just passing through this world as sojourners. In **1 Peter 2:11,** the Apostle Peter tells us that our own passions wage war against us. Paul refers to this also in **Galatians 5:17**.

How then can we live in this world? We live by drawing near to God. We resist the desires of the flesh and thereby do not give in to the natural desires of our physical life. What are those desires? They are the desires of the eyes, the desires of the flesh, and the pride of life, **1 John 2:16. James 4:8 ESV** tells us to "draw near to God and He will draw near to you" and to "resist the devil, and he will flee from you."

Our power to live a Godly and pleasing life is found in the power of the Holy Spirit. That power is ours. We need to seek that power and call upon the name of the Holy Spirit. In Him we will find the strength we need.

"But I say, walk in the Spirit, and you will not gratify the desires of the flesh."
Galatians 5:16 ESV

Think about it. *Selah*

Day Sixty-five: Joshua 1:9

"Have I not commanded you? Be strong and courageous. Do not be frightened, and do not be dismayed, for the Lord your God is with you wherever you go."
Joshua 1:9 ESV

When you face a challenge, you need confidence. When you do something new, you need determination. If you set out to do something that could harm you, it is then that you need leadership. It is then that you must call upon a strength for which you have been prepared, but have not exercised it. If you give in to fear, you will fail. If you allow doubt to gain a foothold, you may quit. You must be strong, and you must act with courage. You must obey all that you have been commanded to do by your coach, your commander, or your leader. When the battle comes, follow your commander to victory. You cannot doubt. You must not give in to fear, but use all that you have been equipped with. Trust your armor, and trust your commander because He cannot lose. You are with Him, and He is with you. He will not fail you, and He will not leave you. He will only encourage you and strengthen you.

When you begin to doubt, remember our hope. When you are taunted by the enemy, remember he is doomed. When you see impending danger ahead of you, then you may be ahead of your commander. Return to Him and follow Him. If you are following God, then wherever you go, He leads you there.
"Have I not commanded you? Be strong and courageous. Do not be frightened, and do not be dismayed, for the Lord your God is with you wherever you go."
Joshua 1:9 ESV Think about it. *Selah*

Day Sixty-six: Matthew 5:9

"Blessed are the peacemakers, for they shall be called sons of God."
Matthew 5:9 ESV

The Colt 45 handgun of the "Wild, Wild West" was called a *peacemaker*. It was developed for the Army but often given credit for helping tame the West where there was little law except for the gun.

Jesus says in **Matthew 5:9** that those who work for peace will be blessed by God and be called for their efforts, "sons of God." They will be associated in the family of God, who is the author of peace, real peace, and lasting peace.

Everywhere Jesus went while on this earth, He brought and offered peace, deliverance, and freedom from the grip of sin and death. He calmed the storms of life and healed the threats of disease. He brought food for the hungry, water for the thirsty, direction for the confused, laughter and joy to the sad and fearful, truth to the seekers, and peace to the troubled. Jesus is the real peacemaker, and we who follow Him are to bring that same peace to those who may cross our way, and to those to whom God may lead us. We bring the Good News of redemption to the world, and that Good News has with it a peace that passes all understanding and comprehension.

Unlike the Colt 45 *peacemaker* that helped keep the peace by fear of its ability to bring death, Jesus brings lasting peace and the offer of lasting life, eternal life. As we bring that Good News to others, we are indeed the sons of God. How blessed can we be to be called the sons of the living God!

"Blessed are the peacemakers, for they shall be called sons of God."
Matthew 5:9 ESV

Think about it. *Selah*

Day Sixty-seven: Romans 8:39

"Nor height nor depth, nor anything else in all creation, will be able to separate us from the love of God in Christ Jesus our Lord." **Romans 8:39 ESV**

Can you remember a time in your life when you were separated from your parents as a child? It was a fearful time, wasn't it? Situations such as that bring fear to both parents and child. At that moment we feel helpless, lost, and most vulnerable. In moments like that, we need help.

In the Christian life, there is no need for fear of being separated from God for we know that God will never leave us or forsake us. It is in moments of uncertainty that we can be certain our God knows where we are, His eye is upon us, and He will not lift His protective hand from us. Nothing can separate us from the love of God that is in Christ Jesus, our Lord and God's Son. There is nothing too big, nothing too wide, nothing within this world or universe, no power, no force, no threat, and no opposition at all that can overcome the supremacy of God's great love for us.

Remember when the disciples were in a boat at night crossing the Sea of Galilee and a great storm suddenly came up and threatened to sink the boat, the very boat where Jesus was asleep? They woke up Jesus and reprimanded Him by saying, "Can't you see what is happening? Don't you care about us? We're about to die!" Well, Jesus did care. He was in the same boat as they were, and He knew He was not about to die. He was about to calm their storm. He had no fear, but He did have peace to offer and calm to bring to their present lives, which He delivered. They were in a storm, but the storm had not separated them from Jesus' love for them. He did care. He did love them. There was nothing that could separate His love for them from them. The height of the wave, the depth of the swell, and the power of the wind were all servants to the voice of Jesus. He is the creator, the sustainer, the life giver, and the Savior. He was with them, and He would not allow anything to come between Him and His children.

Do you realize that this is not just a story? This is a pattern. It is a model and an example of how Jesus presently works in your life. When things happen in your life, do not fear or be afraid for God is with you. He cares for you and has already prepared for this very moment in your life. Believe His promise to you, trust His way with you, and do not doubt. That doubt will only bring confusion and trouble in your life. Choose peace and take God's hand.

"Nor height nor depth, nor anything else in all creation, will be able to separate us from the love of God in Christ Jesus our Lord." **Romans 8:39 ESV**

Think about it. *Selah*

Day Sixty-eight: 2 Timothy 1:7

"For God gave us a spirit not of fear but of power and love and self-control."
2 Timothy 1:7 ESV

Automatic pilot and cruise control are features that can be used to allow a plane to fly on its own. We use cruise control in our cars to allow the car to maintain a consistent speed on its own. They are types of "self-control." These options are benefits to us, and they relieve some of the stress in traveling. They bring comfort to our lives. We also have navigation tools where we can set a destination and they will guide us every mile of the way.

The believer has within him a cruise mechanism based upon the Holy Spirit that brings peace if we engage it. We need to set the course and let the Holy Spirit work. We can draw upon the Holy Spirit.

This self-control is a confidence of "sound judgment." We are told to test the spirits in **1 John 4:1** to see if they are of God or not. If we are unsure, then we need to ask God for more wisdom to gain understanding and direction, and He will give it to us **(James 1:5)**.

There is confidence we can have in our judgment and our self-control, and we can, therefore, live in contentment and peace rather than fear.

Is there something that is bringing fear in your life right now? Engage the tool and live your life your life by it. Allow God to work in your life and have no fear.

"For God gave us a spirit not of fear but of power and love and self-control."
2 Timothy 1:7 ESV

Think about it. *Selah*

Day Sixty-nine: John 1:3

"All things were made through him, and without him was not anything made that was made." **John 1:3 ESV**

In **Genesis** we read that in the very beginning of the beginning, there was God. God was before the beginning. Now that is an awesome thought and one that cannot be fathomed by mankind. Why? It is because we cannot understand *before* a beginning, yet the very word *beginning* suggests that something was there to initiate the start. In a car race, we hear the words, *"Gentlemen and ladies, start your engines!"* The race is about to begin. We also understand the words, *"On your mark. Get set. Go!"* To start a race, to begin a game, or to get something going, there must be someone to command the start.

One characteristic of God is that He is eternal. By that we mean He has no beginning or end. It is a little easier for me to understand never ending, but never beginning is something I have to just accept by faith. A. W. Tozer put it this way, "The reason we cannot understand the Creator God is that we have a 'creature' mind and with that creature mind it is completely impossible to understand 'Creator' thoughts."

God is the prime mover, the beginner, the first and the last. There is nothing ahead of Him or before Him. God also is a three-in-one God; that is, there are three distinct persons, and those three persons make up the one God. We refer to those personalities as the Trinity or the Triune God. The Trinity consists of God the Father, God His Son Jesus, and God the Holy Spirit. They are all God; they are three in one. Jesus prayed for His followers to be united as one as He, the Father, and the Holy Spirit are one.

In **Genesis 1:26 ESV** God said, *"Let us make man in our image."* They were all there, and here in **John 1:3 ESV** we read, *"All things were made through him, and without him was not anything made that was made."* The Great Creator of all things is Jesus Christ, the Word. It was by the Word and His word that came the command for creation to begin, *"'Let there be light,' and there was light."* **Genesis 1:3 ESV**

Jesus made all things and having made all things good, Satan inserted sin. Because of that, Jesus made all things new. He made us a new creation and has a new earth, a New Jerusalem, where we will worship, and a new heaven that will never be touched by Satan. All the new will be made by Him and without Him, nothing in the new heaven or new earth will be made.

You, my friend, are a new creation made by the creative hand of God and especially made to worship God forever and ever throughout all eternity. All the old things will have passed away, and all things will be made new. If you have been made new, then there is no hint of sin within you for the Father has given you the righteousness of Jesus. Don't try to figure it out. It is beyond our *creature* mind's ability to understand. Just thank God for it, because it is all His idea after all.

Think about it. *Selah*

Day Seventy: Exodus 20:3

"You shall have no other gods before me." **Exodus 20:3 ESV**

When we write the name of Jehovah God, we use the upper case *G*. When we refer to anything other than Him, we use the lower case *g*. Why is that so? It is because there is only one God, and there are many other little gods in our lives and in this world. God is eternal. He always *was*. Other gods are made. We give gods a face, a shape, a place and a purpose. We cannot see God. He is the creator of all. God is a spirit. Nothing can contain Him, yet He lives in our hearts. His desire is to be glorified, to be honored, to be talked to, and to be obeyed. We dictate what our little gods do and where they are allowed. God *is*. When Moses asked God what He was supposed to say when the people asked what God's name was, God said, *"I AM WHO I AM."* **Exodus 3:14**

I AM is who He is, and beside Him there is no other. We are not to put any other thing or person before Him for they are all unworthy. God is God. He alone is God. Everything else has been created. Only God is eternal. Non-believers do not know any differently, and it is sad that believers, who do know differently, must be reminded and commanded not to put anything before God, for when we do, we make that a god.

"You shall have no other gods before me." **Exodus 20:3 ESV**

Think about it. *Selah*

Day Seventy-one: Matthew 5:10

"Blessed are those who are persecuted for righteousness' sake, for theirs is the kingdom of heaven."
Matthew 5:10 ESV

Persecution is an everyday thing, not an unusual or a once in a while thing. Jesus informed His followers that we would be persecuted because we are His followers **(John 15:18-20)**. Someone might say that Jesus did not say forgive those who persecute you and say all manner of evil against you for my sake because persecution *might* happen, but because it *will* always happen. People say bad things because we live on a bad earth. This is not heaven. It is earth. The most hurtful thing for the believer suffering persecution is when fellow believers persecute other believers. Why would this happen? It happens when a believer gets his eyes off the righteousness of Jesus, and places them on things of this earth. If we desire to please God, we will not be complaining because of earthly conditions and provisions.

The point here is that persecution is real. It is common, it is every day, and it is to be expected. If it is to be expected, we should be prepared for it. The response for persecution should be to bless those who persecute you for being a follower of Christ and to love your enemies and do good to those who hate you **(Luke 6:27-28)**.

When persecution comes, do good to those who persecute you. By the way, it makes them mad. It bothers them. The reason for this is conviction. The reason for your blessing them is your reward, the kingdom of heaven. Keep your eye on the reward, not the persecution.

"Blessed are those who are persecuted for righteousness' sake for theirs is the kingdom of heaven." **Matthew 5:10 ESV**

Think about it. *Selah*

Day Seventy-two: Isaiah 40:31

"But they who wait for the Lord shall renew their strength; they shall mount up with wings like eagles; they shall run and not be weary; they shall walk and not faint."
Isaiah 40:31 ESV

I have a huge problem. I hate to wait. I want everything done yesterday. Waiting is not a quality that I have mastered. I am woefully lacking here. It is not that I get mad. I just don't like to wait, and I always prepare for situations where I might be required to wait. I prepare for the moment with "A, Plan B, and Plan C." I want everything to work like a clock, a working clock.

My problem, my issue with waiting, is the unknown, not knowing the outcome or how things will work out. I want to know. I don't want there to be any doubt. I want to have assurance about the conclusion of the matter. I want everything to be in place and running smoothly. I want to be prepared and to have everything and everyone in motion doing their part to keep this machine going.

The reason I go to a store is to buy something, not to look. I already know what I want and where it is supposed to be located. I know what I want when I go to a restaurant because the information is on the menu. As you can see now, I have a problem with waiting. I have gotten better with this waiting issue though.

I have discovered that waiting is actually a good thing. My wife has no problem with waiting. Since she has no problem with waiting, it means that I must expect to wait. There is a well-known saying, *"Good things come to those who wait."* Patience and suffering are words that are used in the Bible referring to tribulation (**Romans 5:3**). Suffering and tribulation are both brought about by having to wait, and the result is patience. In **James 1:4** we are admonished to let patience work itself out, and in **Romans 12:12** we see that there is a reward for tribulation, which is patience, or *waiting.*

The well-rounded person, the wise person, or the profitable person knows how to wait. Isaiah is saying this also in **Isaiah 40:31**. Waiting brings about added strength for the journey. It adds to our ability a supernatural ability to do miraculous things, unbelievable things. Waiting provides us with endurance for the race, as we are strengthened and able to go beyond our personal ability. It provides the stick-to-itiveness to not quit. We are able to endure when we do not get into a hurry and just *wait.*

"But they who wait for the Lord shall renew their strength; they shall mount up with wings like eagles; they shall run and not be weary; they shall walk and not faint." **Isaiah 40:31 ESV**

Think about it. *Selah*

Day Seventy-three: Ephesians 6:11

"Put on the whole armor of God that you may be able to stand against the schemes of the devil." **Ephesians 6:11 ESV**

Armor is of little value unless we put on all of it. The purpose of armor is to protect in an area that is vulnerable or weak in a battle. It is devised to increase the possibility of success in battle. Now if the soldier does not put on all of his armor and does not put it on the right way, the attack of the enemy is more effective. Armor prevents injury and brings confidence to the soldier.

The believer or follower of Jesus Christ is in a battle and our commander has provided a sure defense and confidence for victory in our battle. It is the "full armor" of God. It is a brand name armor that carries with it the manufacturer's guarantee against failure. This armor, if properly put on and used, cannot be penetrated. The manufacturer knows the weapons used by the enemy and knows the playbook, the strategy, and the scheming plans of warfare that will be used in every situation and will guarantee victory. The requirement is that we must put it *all* on. We must put on the "full armor" **before** we go into battle.

Now, if you are a believer and follower of Christ Jesus, you must also be obedient to the commands of our Commander in Chief. We must prepare for the war by putting on the full armor. Our part in the battle is to *stand,* not attack. The armor is our defense. Jesus is the one on the white horse. He is the Victor, and we are His praise band.

"Put on the whole armor of God that you may be able to stand against the schemes of the devil." **Ephesians 6:11 ESV**

Is your armor on? If so, you will be able to stand, so stand.

Think about it. *Selah*

Day Seventy-four: Romans 8:38-39

"For I am sure that neither death nor life, nor angels nor rulers, nor things present nor things to come, nor powers, nor height nor depth, nor anything else in all creation, will be able to separate us from the love of God, in Christ Jesus our Lord."
Romans 8:38-39 ESV

To be sure is to be confident. To be confident is to be decisive, unwavering, resilient, and able to move with purpose in moments of difficulty. For a confident person, difficulty does not cause moments of indecision or thoughts of failure because he is sure. A confident person is a happy person who is unmoved by opposition or the opinions of others. A confident person can stand. People are at peace around a confident person.   A confident leader creates an environment in which those under his care are confident also.

Life is filled with conflict, but in the conflict there are few individuals that can be described as confident. The believer's confidence is in Jesus Christ and in Him there is peace, there is love, there is deliverance, and there is a great resource for life.

What is it in your life right now that is causing you great concern or bringing about a feeling of uncertainty? Do you believe that Jesus is equipped to deal with that concern? Do you feel that Jesus wants to help you? Jesus has said that He is with us and there is no situation that would cause Him to leave us. **Hebrews 13:5-6** says, *"Don't love money; be satisfied with what you have. For God has said, 'I will never fail you. I will never abandon you.' So we can say with confidence, 'The Lord is my helper,*

so I will have no fear. What can mere people do to me?' "
NLT

Paul writes in **Romans 8:38-39** that he is sure and, therefore, we can be sure and confident in life because there is no situation that may arise that could cause Jesus to leave us or create an environment where we would be outside the protective hand of Jesus and His great love for us. This confidence is based upon the credibility of Jesus Christ, God's only Son. So, don't allow situations to call Jesus a liar and cause you to believe it. Jesus is our rock and our strong tower.

"For I am sure that neither death nor life, nor angels nor rulers, nor things present nor things to come, nor powers, nor height nor depth, nor anything else in all creation, will be able to separate us from the love of God, in Christ Jesus our Lord."
Romans 8:38-39 ESV

Think about it. *Selah*

Day Seventy-five: Psalm 19:14

"Let the words of my mouth and the meditation of my heart be acceptable in your sight, O Lord, my rock and my redeemer." **Psalm 19:14 ESV**

What you think determines what you will eventually say and do. What you say and do is what shapes your reputation. It is the basis for what others think about you. For the believer, his reputation is a reflection of how others see Jesus. How do others see Jesus in you?

I pray this Psalm every day in my morning quiet time. I want my words to be an encouragement to everyone who may cross my path. I want my thoughts to be those that would honor Jesus. I want them to be what is holy and acceptable to Him.

I will have to admit that I fail many times and on many days. When things do not go as I would have them go, I am tempted to express that in an unacceptable way. There are many times that my thoughts are not pure and holy but selfish and unclean. When those times come, I must be quick to draw near to God and ask His forgiveness. If not, there is a drifting away from being the example that God would have me to be. It is at these moments that I again pray, *"Let the words of my mouth and the meditation of my heart be acceptable in your sight, O Lord, my rock and my redeemer."* **Psalm 19:14 ESV**

Think on the good and eternal things of God and not on those things that fail to give Him glory.

Think about it. *Selah*

Day Seventy-six: Philippians 3:8

"Indeed, I count everything as loss because of the surpassing worth of knowing Christ Jesus my Lord. For his sake I have suffered the loss of all things and count them as rubbish, in order that I may gain Christ." **Philippians 3:8 ESV**

"He is no fool who gives what he cannot keep to gain that which he cannot lose," **(Jim Elliot)**. Jim prefaced this statement by saying, "One of the greatest blessings of Heaven is the appreciation of heaven on earth. The things of earth shall all pass away but the Word of the Lord will stand forever."

There is nothing on this earth that can be counted upon or relied upon because they all will pass away **(Matthew 5:18)**. In **1 Peter 1:24-25,** the Apostle Peter writes: *"'all flesh is like grass and all its glory like the flower of grass. The grass withers, and the flower falls, but the word of the Lord remains forever.' And this word is the good news that was preached to you."* **ESV**

With this in mind, focus on this thought: Why are you worried? Is it an earthly thing that is worrying you? Is the thing that worries you beyond your control? If so, it is in God's control. If it is in His control, why would you worry?   Do something about that which is in your control. Having done that, leave the rest to God for you can do nothing about it, and He can. Trust Him.

Secondly, if it is an earthly thing, it will soon fade away, and in the interim God will give you the grace to deal with it. Just consider it loss. Write it off, give it to God, and forget about it.

The things that really matter are those things that you cannot lose. You cannot lose them because they are in God's hand, in His care, and under His supervision. The things of heaven are eternal and secure. The things that God intends for you to possess on this earth are yours, and they, too, are secure until you have finished using them for God's glory. Just count temporary things of no value and prize those things of heaven.

"Indeed, I count everything as loss because of the surpassing worth of knowing Christ Jesus my Lord. For his sake I have suffered the loss of all things and count them as rubbish, in order that I may gain Christ." **Philippians 3:8 ESV**

Think about it. *Selah*

Day Seventy-seven: Ephesians 6:10

"Finally, be strong in the Lord and in the strength of his might."
Ephesians 6:10 ESV

"When I grow up I'm going to be strong like my daddy." Do you remember as a child going up to a heavy object with your dad and the two of you picking that weight up? I remember such times. I remember grunting and making a face of determination while lifting that weight above my head; but it wasn't me, it was my dad. I was strong in the strength of his might. He is the one who brought about success. I used all my might, but mine was not sufficient; and my dad's was. I thought I lifted it, but I did not.

As believers, we are able to accomplish feats only if we stand in the power of God's strength. Our strength is insufficient. Sometimes we think we are the one who accomplished that feat, but it was God.

If God calls us to a mission or a ministry, we ought to go immediately for this is His desire. Our desire should be in line with His desire. He will supply all we need for the call. **Philippians 4:13 & 19**

There are two truths here:

1. Recognize God's activity in our lives and thank Him for His presence and power.
2. Do not look at our lack of ability or strength to accomplish the call. Look at His promised sufficiency and provision, and then obey.

Has God called you to do something? Have you obeyed His call? If you have gained knowledge, where do you take pride? Are your pride and your praise directed inwardly, or do you give God all the glory for what you have gained and acknowledge Him for what He has done in you? Obey Him, thank Him, and praise Him for what He has done! Our strength is in God.

"Finally, be strong in the Lord and in the strength of his might."
Ephesians 6:10 ESV

Think about it. *Selah*

Day Seventy-eight: Colossians 3:23

"Whatever you do, work heartily, as for the Lord and not for men."
Colossians 3:23 ESV

Have you ever been involved in something that seemed as though it had no value? You think, "What's the purpose here?" I have. After becoming involved, I began to wonder what the real purpose was, and it became hard to work heartily in that commitment. It started out with purpose, but the goal was never really achieved because the goal was unclear. Apparently I was not the only one who felt that way, and the ministry was dropped.

Paul writes to the believer here in **Colossians 3:23** that in whatever we become involved, we should not just be involved, but be totally involved, and do it because we love God and not because of loyalty to an individual. If we become involved in anything spiritual or physical, we should be totally given to the task and give it our all. The question is, "Is it of God?"

This is not to say we should withhold testing the activities in which we are involved. We should test them to see if they are really of God. **1 Thessalonians 5:16-18 ESV** says, *"Rejoice always, pray without ceasing, give thanks in all circumstances; for this is the will of God in Christ Jesus for you."* Test them and ask God to work all the things together for His glory and our good.

Are you involved in something that you are having difficulty being excited about or that you have questions about? Test the activities to see if they are of God, and while you are testing, do the work well. Do it as though

Jesus was visibly there working with you. Work heartily until God gives you further direction.

"Whatever you do, work heartily, as for the Lord and not for men."
Colossians 3:23 ESV

Think about it. *Selah*

Day Seventy-nine: Ephesians 6:12

"For we do not wrestle against flesh and blood, but against the rulers, against the authorities, against the cosmic powers over this present darkness, against the spiritual forces of evil in the heavenly places." **Ephesians 6:12 ESV**

How can people do the terrible, horrific and unthinkable acts that we read about and see and hear in the media today? What would bring a person who was born a beautiful, bright, and loving baby to become a terror and blight against all humanity? It is not the person, the form or the image that we see. It is all the things that we do not see. Our battle and fight on earth is not with the flesh and human blood. These are mere tools that are used by the unseen world, the mighty powers of darkness that are alive and active in our world. They are wicked forces that are even warring against heaven and God Himself. They have taken territory, and they are using human beings as tools to carry out their devilish schemes.

It is hard for us not to focus on the tool rather than the power. Jesus came to redeem, to forgive, and to love these *tools* of humanity, and we need to realize that. The battle is not against people and nations but against Satan and his spiritual forces of darkness.

The end of the matter is already settled. Jesus saves and He has conquered Satan, sin, and the grave. The verdict has been read, the sentencing has been made, and all that is to be done is to carry it out on the set date. Only God knows that date. It is coming. We must only be found faithful doing what God has called us to do, which is to carry his Good News of redemption to the flesh and blood who are held captive.

"For we do not wrestle against flesh and blood, but against the rulers, against the authorities, against the cosmic powers over this present darkness, against spiritual forces of evil in the heavenly places." **Ephesians 6:12 ESV**

Think about it. *Selah*

Day Eighty: John 1:12

"But to all who did receive him, who believed in his name, he gave the right to become children of God." **John 1:12 ESV**

I was taught from childhood to stand up for your rights. The Declaration of Independence proclaims that "all men are created equal, that they are endowed by their Creator with certain unalienable Rights." An unalienable right is a right that cannot be denied, repudiated, or given to another person. It cannot be taken away. Here in John we see that all men have been given a right to become adopted sons of God! It tells us that this right is given in turn for believing that Jesus is who He says He is, who is the only begotten Son of God. Having done this, or having been convinced and publicly proclaiming your understanding and commitment to it, you have been endowed by your Creator to be a new creation, a "son" of God. You now have the right that is unalienable in that it cannot be taken away, and there is nothing more that can be added to it. It is complete.

I guess we could write this: All new creations of God are created equal and are endowed by their Creator with the unalienable right to be called the sons of God, among which is eternal life, liberty, freedom, and genuine, total, and eternal happiness.

"But to all who did receive him, who believed in his name, he gave the right to become children of God." **John 1:12 ESV**

If you do not have this right, you can have it today. Receive Jesus as your Savior by admitting that you are a sinner, hopeless, and without help; believe and trust upon His holy name that Jesus will forgive you of your sins, your past sins, present sins, and all those sins of your future earthly life. If you would do this, then you would be given the right to be called a son of God.

Think about it. *Selah*

Day Eighty-one: Philippians 3:7

"But whatever gain I had, I counted as loss for the sake of Christ." **Philippians 3:7 ESV**

Have you ever worked for something that you thought you wanted, and when you finally were able to buy it, you discovered that it was not what you thought it to be? There are many people who work hard to achieve a goal in life and sadly discover that the gloss had faded and the real joy in life had passed them by. We discover that the important things in life had been overlooked in our rush to gain glory, and what we thought was glorious was so empty. It was only a facade.

Luke writes in **Acts 20:24** about how Paul, as he was leaving for Jerusalem, expressed that life is worth little, or of any real value, unless we use it for doing the ministry that God has called us to do. Here in **Philippians 3:7,** Paul writes to the church at Philippi that things that are of value, things in our lives that can be treasured, lose their value and are not to be treasured after all when we stand them up to the glory of Christ Jesus.

"But whatever gain I had, I counted as loss for the sake of Christ."
Philippians 3:7 ESV

Why not re-evaluate your life to see if you have been looking at life with an eye on eternity? What are the things that are really important in life? I believe all of us need to do a re-evaluation from time to time.

Think about it. *Selah*

Day Eighty-two: Matthew 5:11

"Blessed are you when others revile you and persecute you and utter all kinds of evil against you falsely on my account." **Matthew 5:11 ESV**

No one wants to have lies spread about them. Everyone desires to be treated fairly. To be publicly humiliated, especially when there is no truth to it, is hard to take. We all want truth to prevail in all things, and for sure we should not be a party to anything done unfairly.

Why would someone treat another person in an evil and false manner? I feel it is because of the desire of power over another. When one person cannot have his way, he devises all manner of evil methods to get power. To be treated unfairly and unjustly is for sure not a blessing.

Jesus puts forth a situation here in **Matthew 5:11** where He says that it is a blessing to be unjustly treated by others. That specific situation is when the followers of our Lord Jesus Christ, who believe and trust in Him and have turned over their lives to His care and direction, are singled out by unbelievers and are falsely persecuted. How is that a blessing? It is a blessing because it is for the sake of Jesus. Jesus came to take all the sin of humanity and purify it. He wants to take that which is meant for evil and turn it into good. Jesus came into the world to save sinners, and our job is to proclaim that Good News. If we are persecuted in proclaiming it, we are treated as they treated Jesus (**John 3:16; 15:18; 16:32**).

Are you glad to sacrifice for your family? Sure you are. Would you gladly take the abuse from another for the sake of your family? I am certain that you would, and you would consider it a blessing. This is what Jesus is saying. It is a blessing, and you have a reward that cannot be revoked and is secure in heaven. Believers today are no different than those of yesterday, and they suffered, as did Jesus.

Expect abuse, expect suffering, and know that you will be called upon to sacrifice; but this earth is not the end. Jesus is worth it, and heaven is eternal. Remember when you are treated unfairly that this too will pass.

"Blessed are you when others revile you and persecute you and utter all kinds of evil against you falsely on my account." **Matthew 5:11 ESV**

Think about it. *Selah*

Day Eighty-three: Exodus 20:12

"Honor your father and your mother, that your days may be long in the land that the Lord your God is giving you." **Exodus 20:12 ESV**

Do you want to live a long life and a life that is full of blessing? Of course you do; and since you do, one way to secure that type of life is to honor your parents, respect your parents, and give allegiance to them.

Mark Twain is given credit for saying, "When I was a boy of fourteen, my father was so ignorant I could hardly stand to have the old man around. But when I got to be twenty-one, I was astonished at how much the old man had learned in seven years." Parents are given the responsibility of raising their children up in the ways of the Lord, to guide them into becoming a follower of Christ Jesus and a blessing to society. Sadly, most parents do not have this as a goal. The fifth commandment is the first one concerning how we are to relate to others, and it begins with the relationship we are to have with our parents.

The first four commandments have to do with our relationship with God:
1. Do not have any other gods before God;
2. Do not worship idols;
3. Do not use God's name in vain; and
4. Keep the Sabbath day holy.

The remaining six commandments have to do with the way we treat others. The lawyer acknowledged this in response to Jesus in **Luke 10:27** when Jesus asked the lawyer to quote the law. The lawyer's response was, *"You* *shall love the Lord your God with all your heart and with all your soul and with all your strength and with all your mind, and your neighbor as yourself."*

We cannot treat others right unless we treat our parent's right. Treating our parents with the respect and honor they deserve is a pattern in how we treat others. To treat others right makes for a long life, a happy life, and a life that is admired by those who observe us.

"Honor your father and your mother, that your days may be long in the land that the Lord your God is giving you." **Exodus 20:12 ESV**

Think about it. *Selah*

Day Eighty-four: Titus 1:2

"In hope of eternal life, which God, who never lies, promised before the ages began." **Titus 1:2 ESV**

A promise is only as good as your good name and the dependability of your truthfulness. Trust and hope are only as reliable as your word and character. The hope of the believer is in Jesus Christ, God's only begotten Son. He is the Truth, and He is faithful, He is reliable, He is dependable, and He is our Rock upon which our trust is built.

Jesus is God, and God cannot lie (**Numbers 23:19**). Upon the righteousness of His character, He said He is going to prepare a place for us and that He will come again just as He went away; therefore, the truth is that a believer has eternal life, period. We have eternal life promised to us for taking Jesus Christ as our Savior and Redeemer. In exchange for that, we can expect to live with Christ Jesus for eternity in heaven.

Do you believe that? If you do, you have no reason to doubt someone who has promised you eternal life. If you have doubt, who do you think is causing this doubt? It is not God, because He cannot lie. I would say it is a liar and the father of all lies. It is Satan (**John 8:44**) and his followers who are spreading such lies.

"In hope of eternal life, which God, who never lies, promised before the ages began."
Titus 1:2 ESV

Think about it. *Selah*

Day Eighty-five: Deuteronomy 6:4

"Hear, O Israel: The Lord our God, the Lord is one." Deuteronomy **6:4 ESV**

Jehovah God, the Great I AM is a God of unity. God is one. He is not divided. When Jesus prayed for us before His crucifixion, He asked of the Father that His disciples and His followers today would be just like He and the Father are one, **John 17:11**. When Philip asked Jesus to show the disciples the Father, Jesus' response was that if you have seen Him then you have seen the Father, **John 14:8-9**. The Father, the Son, and the Holy Spirit are one. They are three but one, three in one. We call this the Trinity.

God has nothing to do with division, discord, or the party spirit. All those things are of this world's system and worldview. Where the Spirit of the Lord is, there is freedom, and unity, **Ephesians 4:4-5; 2 Corinthians 3:6**.

One more thing: God does not contradict Himself for He is truth, and you can trust Him.

"'Hear, O Israel: The Lord our God, the Lord is one.' " Deuteronomy **6:4 ESV**

Think about it. *Selah*

Day Eighty-six: Titus 1:1

"Paul, a servant of God and an apostle of Jesus Christ, for the sake of the faith of God's elect and their knowledge of the truth, which accords with godliness,"
Titus 1:1 ESV

Paul was a servant, an apostle, and an example and pattern for us as believers to follow. He lived a model life for the benefit of believers. Paul wanted to be an encouragement as well as an example for believers for the sake of their faith in Christ Jesus. Not only did he want to be a "go-to" person for followers of Christ, but he wanted to be a professor of truth and a fitness trainer for the godly life in Christ Jesus.

This is the type of life that believers today should aim to develop. Life is not really about us; it is about two things, "Him and them." We are third. Tony Dungy who was once a coach of the Indianapolis Colts football championship team said his desire in life was like that of Paul and his ambition. He writes in his book, **Mentor Leader**, *"Relationships are ultimately what matter; our relationship with God and with other people . . . What can I do to make other people better, to make them all God created them to be?"*

How do you view life, your life, and the lives of others around you? Do you view yourself as a servant of God, an ambassador, a teacher, a mentor of the truth and a pattern for others to follow? If not, you need to be a mentor or reset your life. It is not about you; it's all about "Him and them."

"Paul, a servant of God and an apostle of Jesus Christ, for the sake of the faith of God's elect and their knowledge of the truth, which accords with godliness,"
Titus 1:1 ESV

Think about it. *Selah*

Day Eighty-seven: Ephesians 6:23

"Peace be to the brothers, and love with faith, from God the Father and the Lord Jesus Christ." **Ephesians 6:23 ESV**

Peace, love and faith, for some reason these characteristics of the Christian life are looked down upon, misunderstood and sometimes shunned by other fellow believers and preachers.

God is love and we ought to preach, teach, and live in a life of love for God and others. Jesus says that He left with us His peace. It was not the same thing that is thought of by the world's standards and definition. It was a real and lasting peace. It was eternal peace that could not be forfeited, lost, or replaced. Peace is not weakness. It can only be offered and kept by power. Weakness brings insecurity and failure. Peace and love bring tranquility, confidence, and joy in life. It is what secures our faith, hope, and trust.

This is what Jesus brings, and it is what ought to be introduced into the environment in which the believer is injected. The believer is not in this world to bring about conviction. That is the work of the Holy Spirit. The responsibility of believers is not to bring political reform but life reform and life in Christ more abundantly. Ravi Zacharias has said, "Jesus did not come into this world to make bad people good. He came to make dead people live."

Be all about peace, love, and faith before others. Preach it, teach it, live it, and most of all, never be ashamed of it for it is what the Gospel of Christ brings.

"Peace be to the brothers, and love with faith, from God the Father and the Lord Jesus Christ." **Ephesians 6:23 ESV**

Think about it. *Selah*

Day Eighty-eight: Deuteronomy 6:7

"And you shall teach them diligently to your children, and shall talk of them when you sit in your house, and when you walk by the way, and when you lie down, and when you rise." **Deuteronomy 6:7 ESV**

At the time of this writing, I am sixty-eight years old. I get great satisfaction in reminiscing over the adventures that my wife and I had in raising our three children. These memories bring a smile to my face, joy to my heart, and glory to my great God. God has been so very faithful. It is not just the memories. There are also things happening today and things that will be happening tomorrow that our grandchildren are bringing and will bring into our lives.

The reason for the happiness in the adventures and events is that we experienced teaching them about Jesus. It was not a classroom situation with desks, chairs, and a writing board. It was what happened as we lived. Life gave us the opportunity to inject truth, apply Biblical principles, and give reprimand and guidance that would bring security to their future lives.

In **Proverbs 22:6,** Solomon writes that the goal of a parent and grandparent is to train up a child in the way that he should go. If we do that, when he gets grown he will stick to that training and will not leave those teachings and foundational truths. This verse is often misunderstood. A better way of putting it would be to help our children find their bent in life, or God's Will in their life. We need to help them discover what it is that God has for them. If we do and they discover it, they will be strengthened by the Holy Spirit to remain in that bent and will not depart from it. This is not just taking them to church and Christian events; it is a day-by-day, hour-by-hour job. It is making life meaningful and God applicable to them in life. It is to help them see God and see themselves in God's hand. It takes diligence on the parents' and grand-parents' part to achieve this goal.

The joy for us in the future is the memory of God's faithfulness to us as we traveled down the road.

"And you shall teach them diligently to your children, and shall talk of them when you sit in your house, and when you walk by the way, and when you lie down, and when you rise." **Deuteronomy 6:7 ESV**

Think about it. *Selah*

Day Eighty-nine: Genesis 2:1

"Thus the heavens and the earth were finished, and all the host of them."
Genesis 2:1 ESV

What God starts, He finishes; and He does all things well. There is nothing that He cannot do well. Is anything too hard for God? I think not. **Jeremiah 32:17 & 27:** *'Ah, Lord God! It is you who have made the heavens and the earth by your great power and by your outstretched arm! Nothing is too hard for you.' . . . 'Behold, I am the Lord, the God of all flesh. Is anything too hard for me?* **ESV**

Never try to put yourself in the place of God or to put God in your shoes. What would Jesus do? Jesus would do things right. Jesus would follow through. Jesus would leave nothing undone. We cannot be God; but God did come as a man, and when He did, He did all things well.

Since we cannot be God, we must seek His direction, seek His will, and be faithful in finishing what He has called us to do. If we do things through Christ Jesus, then all things are made possible for us. *"With man this is impossible, but with God all things are possible,"* **Matthew 19:26**. The desire of the believer is to want to finish the race and finish well. That takes determination, faithfulness, and reliance upon God on our part. (**Philippians 3:14**)

Think about it. *Selah*

Day Ninety: Exodus 20:8

"Remember the Sabbath day, to keep it holy."
Exodus 20:8 ESV

What is the Sabbath day? If we do not have this information, what is there to remember, and how can we keep it holy? In **Genesis 2:1-3** we read the summary of the creative work of God: *"So the creation of the heavens and the earth and everything in them was completed. On the seventh day, God had finished his work of creation, so he rested from all his work. And God blessed the seventh day and declared it holy, because it was the day when he rested from all his work of creation."* **NLT**

Here in **Exodus 20:8,** we have the giving of the Law by God, and the fourth command by God was to remember the Sabbath day and to remember that it was the day that He completed His work of creation. It was the day when there was nothing left to do because everything was very good. It was excellent, so He stopped. It was God Himself who set it apart from all the other days as being a holy day. It was to be a holy day, a day of rest, a day of remembrance of God's good deeds to us and for us, and a day of celebration for God and God alone.

Having remembered all this we should keep this day of rest as a special day, a day that is different from all others, and a day that was made for mankind's benefit and well-being. Jesus reminded the religious leaders regarding the Sabbath in **Matthew 12:8** that He, the Son of Man, was the ruler of the Sabbath and in **Mark 2:27** *"And he said to them, 'The Sabbath was made for man, not man for the Sabbath.'"* **ESV**

Jesus is Lord; He is the one to be praised, celebrated, worshiped, and remembered on the Sabbath. The Sabbath was given to man as a blessing, not a burden.

After Jesus rose from the grave, He met with His disciples on the first day of the week as they met **(John 20: 19 & 26)**. After Jesus ascended into heaven, we read in **Acts 20:7** that it was the first day of the week that the early church designated to meet for worship, and it became the Christian Day of Worship, or the day that they set aside (a Sabbath) for rest, remembrance, and worship.

Therefore, let me ask you: What are you doing Sunday? May I encourage you to be dedicated to your local body of believers, your local church, and when out of town, seek out Bible-believing followers of Christ and be joined with them in church on the Lord's Day.

A friend of mine has this commitment for his choir members: *"When in town, be in church, be in choir, be at practice."* **David Willard**

"Remember the Sabbath day, to keep it holy." **Exodus 20:8 ESV**

Think about it. Selah